FREE·
HEEL
SKIING

FREE·HEEL SKIING

TELEMARK AND PARALLEL TECHNIQUES FOR ALL CONDITIONS

SECOND EDITION

PAUL PARKER

THE
MOUNTAINEERS
Seattle, Washington

Bâton Wicks
London

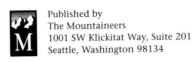
Published by
The Mountaineers
1001 SW Klickitat Way, Suite 201
Seattle, Washington 98134

Second edition: first printing 1995, second printing 1996, third printing 1997

Manufactured in the United States of America

Edited by Kathleen Larson Florio
Illustrations by Steve McDonald
Cover design by The Mountaineers Books
Book design, layout, and typesetting by The Mountaineers Books

Cover photograph: Front: *Michael Wheeler, Chamonix, France;*
    Back: *Mt. Baker, Washington* (Photos: Ace Kvale)
Frontispiece: *Franziska Witmer-Shapiro flying in fluff* (Photo: Mark Shapiro)
Opposite table of contents: *Quit clowning around, Bernie (Rob Bernthal and John Falkiner)*
    (Photo: Mark Shapiro)
Photo credits: Ace Kvale (pp. 8, 12, 16-17, 24, 31, 44–45, 76, 95, 97, 139, 161, 168, 184);
    Kenneth Redding (pp. 102–103, 106, 121); Enzo Ruffino (pp. 78–79);
    Mark Shapiro (pp. 34, 40, 55, 65, 83, 100, 111, 119, 130–131, 147, 159, 175)

Library of Congress Cataloging-in-Publication Data
Parker, Paul, 1953–
    Free-heel skiing : telemark and parallel techniques for all conditions / Paul Parker ;
[illustrations by Steve McDonald]. — 2nd ed.
        p.   cm.
    Includes bibliographical references and index.
    ISBN 0–89886–412-7
    1. Telemark (Skiing).   2. Telemark (Skiing)—History.   I. Title.
    GV854.9.T44P37   1995
    796.93—dc20   95–12628
                                                                                    CIP

Published simultaneously in Britain by Bâton Wicks, London.
    All trade inquiries U.K. and Commonwealth (except Canada) to Cordee, 3a De Montfort
    Street, Leicester, LE1 7HD, England

ISBN 0-898573-06-9 (UK)

British Cataloguing-in-Publication Data
    A catalogue record for this book is available from the British Library

Two special thanks

Grazie, Nanni
Thanks, Roanne

CONTENTS

FOREWORD

Until I started watching and listening to Paul Parker, I had pretty much taught myself to ski by just going out and doing it. I have short, strong legs and had done enough backcountry skiing to get pretty good at survival turns.

I was introduced to cross-country skis and the telemark turn about twelve years ago by Doug Robinson and his band of "Armadillos" on the east side of the Sierra. At the time, I couldn't understand why they insisted on messing with the pine tar and klister and zigzagging around instead of simply slapping on some skins and going straight up the hill. And those weird drop-knee turns! Why not just parallel or do survival stem christies?

A few years later I found myself coming down Denali pulling a fifty-pound sled through eighteen inches of heavy new snow. I put the load on my back, thinking I could easily ski this stuff on my alpine touring skis, but soon realized that with the load, the wet snow, and the floppy mountain boots there was no way I could begin to initiate a turn. So I unlatched my heels and headed down with a sort of snowplow/stem/telemark/steering turn. No unweighting was necessary or possible. This experience was a revelation to me and soon afterwards I hung up my fat boards and went skinny.

Corn was the new diet. A typical morning in May or June might find me hiking up some slope in the Tetons or Absarokas, maybe sitting on top for an hour or so to let the corn become velvet, then cutting down in wide, classic telemarks.

But it was while skiing with Artie Burrows, Julie Neils, and Murray Cunningham in Aspen that my eyes were first opened to the full potential of skinny skis. Not only were these people outskiing nearly everyone on the mountain regardless of gear, but theirs was not the Peruvian-hat, double-poling, Al Jolson-mammy-turn technique I had known. These jaded ex-alpine racers were blending the old with the new to create an entirely original sport. I was stoked, but I had some work to do! This is about the time I started to really watch and listen to Paul Parker.

Paul is my kind of instructor. He gives me a one-sentence technique

Michael Wheeler doing snow study in Kasmir

9

tip, then leaves me alone until he sees that I've digested it. I have been given more than a few tips by him over the years while skiing *toute neige-toute* in various off-beat parts of the world as we've traveled together testing equipment.

There was a day in Steamboat, skiing hardpack, paralleling the steep stuff, and telemarking the intermediate hills. I'd always had trouble with my left-hand teles and Paul told me to think about pressing the little toe of my back foot against the slope. This worked to get my feet closer together and my skis on edge and corrected my habit of going into my left turns from a stem.

A few days later, a foot of heavy, skied-out cement in Breckenridge stopped me cold. Paul told me to exaggerate my ups and downs the way skiers used to do before high-top plastic boots. This worked, too.

In Hokkaido we met up with fifteen members of the 200-member Japanese Telemark Association. None of them had skied outside Japan, and they were anxious to watch Parker to see if they were on the right track. They were all excellent skiers on the pistes, skiing in perfect Austrian feet-locked-together style. No yelling, and no smiling. When it snowed a meter we headed for the trees—all birch and giant bamboo—and Paul gave me a powder tip. He told me to pretend to grip a pencil between my hip and waist. This got my skis off to the side and together. Switching from side to side got the powder rhythm going and I made five or six good turns before I blew it. Not bad, though. Nor were the Japanese much better in the powder. I sensed them wondering why we didn't just go back to those nicely packed slopes.

The next day Paul told me not to let my hand drop down and back. As soon as I planted my pole, the other hand came forward. "Let out a big, aggressive grunt every time you do a turn," he said. I did this and suddenly it all came together—we were like two hooting kamikazes, grunting and screaming through the trees, finally breaking out of the woods and laughing our heads off, covered from head to toe in the white stuff. Very un-Japanese.

I can't always listen to Parker. Sometimes I have to just watch. A few years ago several of us spent a week in the Sierra skiing the peaks north of Mount Whitney. It was late spring and there had been a day of wet snow and rain followed by a couple of cold nights, so when going out over Sheppard's Pass it was no surprise to find the north side a sheet of ice. No way was I going to even attempt traverses or kick turns on that thirty-five degrees of smooth ice. I climbed down the rocks, paralleling the gully as far as I could, and searched through my pack for something sharp and hard to scratch steps when I looked up to see Parker with his forty-pound pack jump-turning down in perfect control. We all watched fairly aghast, when Paul stopped, looked down at his feet, and calmly announced that the bail on one of his experimental bindings had broken on one side. He pushed off again, this time being careful to keep the one ski on the ice so he didn't jump out of the binding. By the time he was safely down I was so shattered that I threw off my heavy pack and watched it whirl down in great leaps for hundreds of feet to the snowfield below. Then I pulled out a couple of tent pegs and started scratching nicks in the ice, lowering myself down on my belly.

"Hey, Paul. Wait for me."

—**Yvon Chouinard**

PREFACE

It's now well over twenty years ago that telemark skiing began a slow rebirth in the United States. When this rebirth started, few young skiers knew about telemark, and many older skiers didn't care to remember it. It was a technique that our parents and grandparents had used before ski lifts, the Arlberg technique, and alpine bindings.

This early wave of telemark skiing started in America's heyday of alpine skiing—Hexcel Sundances; red, white, and blue sweaters; jet sticks; and painful black Langes. The expense, the distasteful, flashy style, and the physical discomfort of alpine skiing—especially painful boots—were good reasons to pursue telemark. But we really didn't need good reasons. Telemark was a beautiful, graceful, functional turn. It felt pure; it was a secret unknown to the masses. The gear was inexpensive, comfortable, and lightweight—even if it didn't afford much control.

Telemark skiing was countercultural. It was a response to the flash of the alpine scene. Telemarkers were usually younger, backcountry skier types, college students, dope smokers, mountaineers. That day's telemark gear gave us access to the backcountry.

Very few alpine skiers knew what telemark skiing was, so they ignored us. We didn't try to ride lifts much, so access wasn't a serious issue. But as tele skiers became more eager to make turns and less eager to climb for them, ski areas felt a need to restrict our access. So for a few years ski areas limited what terrain we could use. I remember trying to go helicopter skiing in the Canadian Bugaboos with my tele skis and being turned away by Canadian Mountain Holiday's Austrian guides.

Racing helped give telemark skiing some exposure and, eventually, acceptance at ski areas. Races were organized opportunities to dress up in old clothes, run a few gates, and, mostly, enjoy a three-day party.

But racing changed over time. Hotshots from all over the United States, and eventually from Scandinavia and Europe, congregated at big races. They got more and more serious, kept score, and organized what had once been chaotic and just for fun. It was the inevitable result of people's competitive drive to compare themselves with others. But, unlike what has happened in many other sports, racing didn't come to dominate

Vicheres, Switzerland

13

telemark. A few people followed the racing scene religiously, but most chose not to. In the United States it's still all-round skiing on- and off-piste that drives the sport. That's what this book is about.

In those early days of telemark it was the mystery that kept it going. Today, we're skiers like many others—the sport is accepted. But look around, and although you'll see more tele skiers than in years back, somehow it still holds a bit of that mystery. We are in the minority. I like that.

This book is a culmination of twenty-odd years of free-heel skiing and teaching. That sounds like a long time, but I still love the sport. When I went skiing for the first time this season, I was so excited that I couldn't sleep the night before. Skiing still does that for me. I hope it does that for you.

Throughout this book I've used the term *free-heel* with skis, skiers, and skiing. *Free-heel* is an inclusive term that also points to the most essential difference between skiers who use alpine and skiers who use nordic equipment. Backcountry, cross-country, and telemark skiers and equipment are free-heel. This book is written for those skiers, whether they're at the beginner, intermediate, or expert level.

How should you use the information in this book? If you are a beginner, pick the section that applies to you, and practice. Be patient—build a foundation. You need mileage. I've purposefully been spare in the language because in your case, mileage is more important than words. Look at the pictures. Work on only one tip at a time.

Intermediate and advanced skiers need mileage, too; but we have to be sure that you don't complete that mileage with bad habits. Find the technique and level that apply to your skiing, and start there. Then, when you have some time, read back over the beginning sections.

Once I've moved through the early teaching progressions, most of the techniques in this book are refined through tips, or points of focus. Why? Because it's been my experience in both my own skiing and in teaching others that that's what works. A note of caution: think about these points one at a time—not several at once. I've given you a lot of them so that you get your money's worth, but remember that each tip deserves practice. They aren't meant to be crammed into too short a time. Take these tips one by one.

Think about goals, too. Each winter I set a goal for my skiing. That goal might be skiing a certain tour, a special race, or descending a peak or couloir I've been eyeing. Often my goal has been technique related—learning a new one, perfecting an old one, or ridding myself of a bad one. Of course, there's room for more than one goal, as long as I can see them all the way through. Goals keep me interested. They give me something to look forward to through the winter, and they give me something to work for.

It helps to set a goal, but you don't have to be overly intense about it. I like to set goals that are fun. Having a goal keeps you focused in your learning. Be patient. You've got time. One of the things that I love about skiing is that it's something that one doesn't grow out of.

This book was written for your enjoyment—to help you reach your skiing goals and to have fun in the process!

ACKNOWLEDGMENTS

With special thanks to Paul Peterson, PSIA Nordic Demonstration Team Coach and fellow team member. Paul's editing, teaching experience, technical input, and—especially important—his humor were key to the development of this new edition of *Free-heel Skiing*.

And thanks to Yvon Chouinard, Lito Tejada-Flores, Michael Kennedy, Steve McDonald, Roanne Miller, Carl Scofield, Nanni Tua, members of the PSIA Alpine Demonstration Team, and the members of the PSIA Nordic Demonstration Team.

BEGINNINGS

FREE-HEEL'S ROOTS

The real fathers of the sport were not the men who made a few half-hearted experiments with skis and then abandoned the fickle boards in despair, but those who first proved by solid achievement the wonderful possibilities of the ski.

—Arnold Lunn

Throughout modern ski history one theme recurs—the gradual development of two separate skiing disciplines: alpine and nordic. Early masters of the two schools fought like rival siblings to establish theirs as the superior one. Yet neither style succumbed. Instead, each grew more specialized for its home terrain. Alpine developed sophisticated downhill maneuvers; nordic evolved for cross-country travel.

The rebirth of the telemark has brought these two rivals back onto the same terrain. Yet there is still a distance that separates the two, one that, fortunately for the sport of skiing, is shrinking. What today is only a technical or aesthetic difference began as a heartfelt rivalry a hundred years ago.

The feud between nordic and alpine came late in the sport's development, once ski technique had matured. Long before that, skiing had originated in the far north. Most historians credit Scandinavia with the birth of skiing; but some believe it was introduced in China, not as a means of travel across snow but to support people on peat bogs and mud flats while they collected duck eggs.

Historian Arnold Lunn supports this theory. "Pattens have been employed from time immemorial not only on snow, but for crossing mud, sand, lava. . . . " For most, however, skiing began on snow in Scandinavia. Numerous archeological discoveries in Norway, Sweden, and Lapland substantiate this theory.

Pages 16–17: The old and the new Early skis varied in length and shape and were made from ash, pine, or birch. Some were solid boards with the tips soaked or steamed and turned up. Others were frames of wood covered in leather. Skiers used one long pole, which they dragged as a brake and used as an outrigger. While many skis in the far north were short and wide, a pair of Lapland skis had two different lengths. The shorter ski had a kind of "climbing skin" made from fur for uphill purchase; the longer ski was used for glide. Farther south, skis were long, and the two skis in a pair were of equal length, resembling skis used in the 1930s.

THE NORWEGIAN TECHNIQUE

Sondre Norheim is considered the father of the Norwegian technique. It was Norheim who, in the late 1800s, developed the telemark on the slopes around his town of Morgedal in the Telemark region of Norway. He introduced the telemark to the world at a jumping competition in Oslo in 1868, where he not only awed a large crowd with his 76-foot jump but also punctuated his landing with a graceful telemark turn to a stop.

The telemark turn wasn't just a curiosity but a viable technique for the equipment of the day, which consisted of free heels and wooden skis with no side-cut. In the telemark position one could wedge the forward ski slightly and have the effect of one long, side-cut ski. When properly performed the result was an elegant arc, most often a medium-to-long-radius turn well suited to Norway's moderate terrain and deep snow.

Another significant contributor to this Norwegian school was the explorer Fridtjof Nansen. In 1888 Nansen completed a 500-kilometer journey across southern Greenland and in 1890 published a book about the expedition, *The First Crossing of Greenland.* It was the first widely read account of ski technique, development, and philosophy.

Inspired by the California Gold Rush, the Norwegians took their technique to America. Many emigrating Norwegians stopped en route to California and settled in the Midwest, but one, John A. Thorenson, made it all the way to California. Thorenson was later nicknamed "Snowshoe Thompson" for the mail route he pioneered over the formidable Sierra Nevada. For twenty years he carried mail from California to the Nevada mining camps. The combined weight of his oak skis and the mail on his back sometimes exceeded a hundred pounds.

THE ALPINE TECHNIQUE

Although later bolstered by nationalistic pride, the split between alpine and nordic skiing did have technical roots. The alpine countries of central Europe depended on ski troops for the defense of their mountainous borders. Yet negotiating the Alps, with their steep, unforgiving couloirs and rock-strewn slopes, required a different style of skiing. The alpine school evolved using braking techniques with smaller, more controlled turns.

The Austrian Mathias Zdarsky is most often credited as the father of alpine technique. In his book *Lilienfelder skilauf technik,* Zdarsky documented the snowplow turn he performed on his short, compact skis.

Father or not, it sounds as if Zdarsky must have been a real ass. He vehemently promoted the rift between the alpine and nordic schools and directed personal, vindictive abuse against his colleagues using Norwegian technique in the nearby Black Forest. In retrospect it is amusing. Arnold Lunn referred to the infamous feud as the "Battle of the Bindings."

The bindings *were* different, but unlike today, both alpine and nordic bindings were free-heeled. The early nordic bindings resembled today's cable bindings in that they hinged farther back, under the ball of the foot. The alpine bindings, however, hinged in front of the toe, like a modern randonnée binding. It's no wonder that Zdarsky didn't like telemark turns: anyone who has tried to telemark on randonnée gear knows the desperate insecurity of tiptoeing on the rear foot.

Zdarsky skied with only one long pole. It was Georg Bilgeri, an Austrian colonel, who popularized the use of two shorter poles. Bilgeri checked his speed with his turns, like a modern skier and unlike many monopole skiers who used their "ski stock" as an outrigger. He published his techniques but didn't follow any particular "school" of skiing. Bilgeri suggested that alpine skiers use the strong points of both the Norwegian and alpine schools, describing, for example, the "stembogen," or stem turn—a snowplow turn linked by a diagonal run and inspired by both the snowplow and the telemark.

Zdarsky suffered sour grapes over any fame that Bilgeri might have enjoyed. He was so angered by Bilgeri's description of the stembogen in the book *Der Alpin Skilauf* that he challenged the colonel to a duel. Yes, a duel—with guns—over ski technique. Had the duel been carried out and had Bilgeri been a good shot, the modern relationship between nordic and alpine might be much different.

But it wasn't only Zdarsky who fueled the split between the two techniques. Part of the handiwork belonged to Rudolph Lettner, an Austrian metal worker who put metal edges on his skis to keep them from splintering. Not only did the edges increase the life of his skis, but they gave his turns more carve and less skid.

Hannes Schneider, a student of Bilgeri's, was responsible for developing the so-called Arlberg technique, which used more commitment, more angles of the body. The Arlberg skier stood far forward with upper body rotated. The turns were initiated with a stem. Schneider developed the Arlberg as a system for alpine instruction. He combined telemark and stembogen into his Arlberg turn, an early version of the stem christy. He presented his progression of skills to ski schools in 1912, and it dominated downhill ski instruction worldwide until the 1940s.

Telemark was officially dead, at least for alpine instruction. The techniques split—Arlberg for downhill skiing, telemark for tourers in up-and-down terrain.

POSTWAR DEVELOPMENTS

The Second World War brought skiing as a sport to a standstill. Ironically, for Americans the war set the stage for skiing's future. Since fighting in the mountains of Europe necessitated skiing and mountaineering skills, Minot "Minnie" Dole—who later founded the National Ski Patrol—formed the Eighty-seventh Mountain Infantry Division. The Eighty-seventh was soon renamed to what it is known as today: the Tenth Mountain Division. After the war, surviving veterans of the Tenth Mountain Division returned to start the ski areas, ski schools, ski shops, and ski-manufacturing companies that have turned the sport of American skiing into a viable industry.

Nordic skiing did not see as much development, but alpine grew rapidly. In 1946, the first ski-snowshoe race was held at Arapahoe Basin in Colorado. First prize was a can of beer. In 1950, Aspen hosted a World Cup race. In that same year, Cubco bindings were introduced. Their spring-loaded heel piece held the ski-boot heel securely on the ski. This specialization in equipment set the modern course for alpine skiing as the lift-serviced sport that we know today. Free-heeled bindings remained popular with off-piste skiers and ski mountaineers, but for lift-serviced alpine skiers Cubcos became state-of-the-art.

As alpine skiing grew, many more ski lifts were built. Downhill skiers, confined to paths down resort slopes, soon formed moguls. The Arlberg became a dated technique. Its slow, elegant, exaggerated movements were incompatible with the bump-studded hills. Alpine turns became quicker.

In 1959, Cliff Taylor developed his Graduated Length Method (GLM), a mixed blessing in the development of skiing. Admittedly, it did allow more people to learn the sport more easily; but what had once been nice, round moguls developed into evil little ski-bending bumps. With the development of GLM, many alpine skiers, disgusted by hackers' short skis ruining even the steepest slopes, ventured into the backcountry.

In the early 1970s, in a number of little backcountry pockets around the snowy United States, skiers exhumed the telemark, a technique that brought downhill stability to their free-heeled gear. They could tour off the alpine trails and make sweeping turns in idyllic snow inaccessible to the short alpine skis. They could get back to the sport's beginnings, where many of them thought it should have stayed in the first place. Crested Butte, Colorado, was one of these little pockets where the telemark was reborn. That is where I was first exposed to it.

An important contributor to telemark's rebirth was Rick Borkovek. A longtime resident of Crested Butte who now resides in Aspen, Rick published a number of articles on the tele's comeback that inspired mountaineers and ski tourers to give it a try. Manufacturers were urged to make new products for telemarkers. First they developed plastic-laminated cross-country skis with aluminum edges. These evolved into "skinny alpine skis" with tunable steel edges. As skis got wider, boots got higher and stiffer, first home-modified by the hard-core piste skiers, then factory-made as the demand grew.

In the mid-1970s, the competitive urge and a need for recognition inspired an alpine-style racing series for telemarkers: the Summit Series. First it was just for fun; then it got serious. Racers were required to make telemarks and were penalized for any technical transgressions. Those interested in honing their parallel technique stayed out of the gates—or off the piste.

In 1980, the Professional Ski Instructors of America (PSIA) formed a demonstration team that, in 1983, introduced the modern American telemark and teaching methods to the world at Interski in Sesto, Val Pusteria, Italy. Telemark teaching grew at many ski areas, and the PSIA eventually offered a Nordic Downhill certification.

Free-heel skiing continues to grow. To mountaineers and backcountry skiers telemarking satisfies the special appeal of doing more with less. It is a departure from the norm. It is a challenge. Most important, it is fun.

The Battle of the Bindings has come full circle. Alpine and nordic skiers now carve turns on the same terrain. Accomplished free-heel skiers are mastering alpine techniques. Less popular are the labels, the "schools."

As Nansen wrote, ". . . nothing steels the willpower and freshens the mind as skiing. This is something that develops not only the body but also the soul—it has far deeper meaning for a people than many are aware of. . . ."

Denali

It was a cold, drizzly morning on Denali's Muldrow Glacier. Although we had almost 24 hours of daylight, we were in a hurry to be off before the snow got too soft. Soon we would have to go on the night shift, moving in the evening, when the sun's low arc left long, cold shadows.

Gearing up that morning was epic. It had been like that every day. It was too late to say it, but the problem was the array of equipment we had chosen. Most of the group had prototype randonnée bindings, and there lay the problem: the bindings still had a few bugs. When they worked perfectly they were better than our nordic setup because the stiffer boots and wider skis gave more control. But they never worked perfectly.

Two of us were using old double-Galibier touring boots, the only ones available in 1975. We had edged nordic skis and heavy steel cable bindings. Our equipment was simple—all we had to do was step in, bend over, and flip the front throw. We had none of the others' prereleases, iced binding mechanisms, or hinges to grease. But our system was far from perfect.

High on the mountain, we left our skis behind. It was a good thing we had judged the boilerplate unskiable. The mountain was winning as, one by one, our mountaineering bindings fell apart. Our ugly-duckling nordic gear—nothing fancy, just simple and dependable—held fast. Still, I was relieved by the failures; I didn't want to ski those hard, exposed slopes on any of our gear.

I had expected that since my boots could flex, my feet would be warmer. I had no idea how cold that mountain really was; above 16,000 feet my boots remained frozen solid. I clumped along just like everybody else. We reached the summit in good weather, but it was still brutally cold. My feet were on the edge. I wiggled my toes unconsciously; I couldn't have stopped if I had wanted to. It was the one time I would have gone for a pair of those huge, goofy "mouse" boots. Summit time was brief; a few photos and we started squeaking down, crampons noisy in the cold névé.

The descent down the glacier was long—18 miles—and uneventful. We were so terrified of crevasses we used our skins when descending the lower slopes. Cracks were everywhere, creaking and groaning. Now it was too warm.

Our skis were like snowshoes. I began wondering why we had taken skis at all—because we just didn't know when to quit? Used just for transportation, they were unwieldy and undependable. But I wanted to make them work for mountaineering, to find the gear and adventures that were the ideal match. There was great room for improvement.

FREE-HEEL EQUIPMENT

In the early days of telemark's rebirth, one of life's greatest pleasures could be found on a wide, open powder slope by sticking one ski out in front and letting the silky snow pull it around. Those wooden boards made a subtle, smooth hissing noise in the cold snow.

The ability to turn depended largely on the snow conditions. Skis of laminated wood with lignostone (compressed wood) edges needed the right resistance from the snowpack to bend into an arc. The big gear decision was whether or not to get the half-length, screwed-on "Marius" edges. They increased bite on hard snow but stiffened the already stiff skis, and they added weight. It seemed a bit of a waste since, although we found ourselves desperately thrashing on icy trails getting to our destination, we were really after the soft powder slopes.

Today free-heel skiers cut up every imaginable snow condition. Equipment has evolved to alpine levels of performance. No word describes the recent breakthroughs in free-heel gear except *radical*. Wider skis, plastic boots, sturdier bindings—these are all new developments that I'll describe below.

Some skeptics feel that, in a sport with such traditionalist roots, we are losing the spirit of telemarking and are reinventing alpine skiing. It's up to the individual; for me the spirit of free-heel skiing doesn't have so much to do with the genre of the gear as with the fact that I have free heels. When I'm struggling to stay vertical in breakable crust or mashed potatoes, I don't care much about tradition.

You don't need several sets of gear to enjoy free-heel skiing. Below I'll list some options—different kinds of equipment for different uses. Since this is a book on downhill/nordic techniques, the gear is all downhill-oriented; but most of it is versatile enough to work well in a surprisingly wide variety of terrain and snow.

SKI TERMS

When you choose a pair of skis, you will need to know a little about *side-cut*, *camber*, and *flex*.

Yaaaahh!!!

1

A side-cut ski

2

Camber

Skis for turning need side-cut. In 1861 Sondre Norheim began cutting a concave arch into the sides of his wooden skis. This arch formed a narrower midsection for the skis, called the *waist*, giving them wider tips and tails. These skis were *side-cut*. When body weight is applied to the edge of a side-cut ski, the waist presses down to contact the snow, forming a bend—an arc—in the ski (see illus. 1).

Camber is the concave arch in the center of the ski (see illus. 2). There are two general types of camber, alpine and nordic. You'll hear alpine camber referred to as *single camber* and nordic as *double camber*. I prefer not to use these distinctions because true double camber is the *very* stiff midsection of a classic-style cross-country racing ski. Backcountry skis should never have true double camber; they have a "camber and a half."

Compared with alpine camber, nordic camber creates a more arched and stiffer section in the center of the ski, which forms a wax "pocket." That's the "camber and a half." Kick wax that grips the snow is applied to this area of the ski; the tips and tails are waxed with harder glider wax. The center wax pocket is pushed down onto the snow for purchase. This is the skier's "kick." When gliding, the skier's weight is distributed on the faster, glide-waxed tips and tails.

Alpine and cross-country downhill skis have an alpine camber that distributes weight more evenly over the entire running surface. With the correct alpine camber you get a "rebound" effect from turn to turn. When flexed, alpine-cambered skis should form a smooth arc, with no bumps, wiggles, or wax pockets. When squeezed together base-to-base most alpine-cambered skis are easy to close and have no resistant wax pocket.

Ski *flex* most commonly refers to the longitudinal flexibility of a ski. Flexing skis is like kicking tires—more ritual than fact. Although flex is the easiest thing to test off the snow, it is only one characteristic of a ski.

Flex won't tell you much about a ski's performance; you have to add width and side-cut into the equation.

Traditional thinking says that softer-flexing skis *arc* (flex into a curve to scribe a turn) more easily in softer snow; stiffer skis are more stable and will edge better on hard snow but are slow to turn in powder. These rules of thumb are changing with new constructions that increase torsional rigidity—a ski's resistance to twisting along its long axis. Today, the best-performing all-around skis are very rigid torsionally, with a medium-to-soft overall flex. Even World Cup alpine racing skis flex like this—not too stiff. Telemark racers, skiers who frequent prepared piste, and those who live in climates with very hard snow conditions may choose a stiffer board, but they are the exception among telemark skiers. I prefer soft-to-medium-flexing skis that are very rigid torsionally. Have a knowledgeable salesperson show you a few skis. Getting them on snow is the real acid test, but in the shop you can get an idea of the range of ski flexes that are available.

CHOOSING YOUR GEAR

Before getting into technical specifics I'd like to give you a little advice on gear selection. The assortment of gear described here is oriented toward heavier equipment, more for the powder hound than the trail skier. The trail segment of backcountry skiing offers a wide variety of equipment. But in the mountains, I prefer heavier equipment for touring because it affords much more stability with a pack and better performance in the turns. That's usually why I'm out there—to make turns.

For example, I climb peaks, hut tour, and lift ski in the same pair of high plastic boots. They work best on the downhills, but work fine on the uphills because the cuff has a locking mechanism that allows it to be unlocked to hinge freely. I love the support when I'm carrying a heavy pack in difficult snow. Those who do less downhill and more hut touring, however, might select a lower-model boot or a lighter, shorter ski. It depends on what you plan to do most often.

So, how do you make your choice? Do as much skiing as you can before you buy, decide what kind of skiing you think you will want to do most, and then choose your gear accordingly. If you can, rent before you buy. In areas where telemark skiing is popular you can rent the very best gear. Remember that skis need to be matched to boots, or vice versa. Consult these pages for general knowledge, and then go to a service-oriented specialty shop where you feel you can get good information and work with the salesperson for the gear that best suits your needs.

SKIS

Skis have become more specialized as telemark skiing has evolved. In the following discussion I've tried to keep things as uncomplicated as possible.

General Types of Free-heel Skis

I'll break things down into three general categories of edged, backcountry touring/telemark skis: (1) lighter-weight, edged, nordic-cambered backcountry skis; (2) wider, alpine-cambered telemark skis, and (3) super-wide skis. Each category has a variety of choices for different personal preferences and climates. Choose your category according to where you live and what you plan to do most, and then shop within that category.

I'm leaving out edgeless skis. In the earlier days of telemark skiing, edgeless touring skis—especially side-cut, torsionally rigid ones like the old Epokes—played an important role in the ski quiver of the backcountry skier. But backcountry skiing has evolved so that the lion's share of outback skis are edged—skis designed to turn and hold on a variety of backcountry snows. There are good edgeless skis out there for off-trail backcountry skiing, but I prefer ones with edges for frozen corn and windblown snow.

Edged, Nordic-cambered Backcountry Skis

These are narrower, more traditional versions of backcountry skis, ranging from 55 to 60 millimeters underfoot. They are well suited for lower-topped Norwegian-welt boots (see Boots) or the new sturdier, narrower boot/binding systems. They are designed for long tours in varied terrain that require both kick-and-glide and downhill performance. This type of ski will also work fine for the occasional day of lift skiing at a resort. They should have at least 10 millimeters of side-cut and be about 55 millimeters wide at the waist. They should be torsionally rigid for turning stability in all types of snow conditions. Depending on their construction, these skis will weigh around 5 to 6 pounds.

What about *waxless* skis? Waxless models of edged nordic skis are available from some manufacturers. Yes, they are easy to use. But in cold, dry, easy-waxing climates, waxless skis sacrifice glide and turnability for the advantage of not having to bother with wax or skins. Waxless models are best suited for areas with frequent wet and warm conditions which make waxing difficult.

If you feel that you need a waxless ski, look for a negative-patterned base, one that is cut *into* the ski. Stay away from positive waxless patterns

3
A waxlesss
ski base

that protrude beyond the base level of the ski. They are literally a drag and make the skis more difficult to turn (see illus. 3).

Alpine-cambered Telemark Skis

These are wider than the nordic-cambered skis, ranging from 75 to 80 millimeters at the tip and around 60 millimeters underfoot. These are the true telemark skis developed for challenging backcountry downhills and double–black-diamond resort skiing. Most hard-core backcountry powder hounds choose this type of ski. One rule of thumb: the wider the ski, especially in this category, the taller and stiffer the boot you should choose.

The stiffness in the midsection of a nordic-cambered ski interferes with the smooth "line" of the ski that's flexed into an arc for a turn. So if you ski mostly downhill, either using lifts or self-propelled, you will want alpine-cambered tele skis. When pressured and steered into a turn, alpine-cambered skis flex in one smooth arc with no flat spot.

What's the compromise for this downhill performance? On the trail, alpine-cambered skis are slower gliding when waxed. But there are lighter-weight models that are nonetheless suitable for backcountry skiing.

Alpine-cambered skis come in various flexes. They have all grown wider in recent years. Generally speaking, softer ones are for soft snow, stiffer ones for hard snow. New technologies are muddying this distinction, however. You can have a soft, torsionally rigid ski that is easy and quick to turn yet holds on bulletproof snow. Generally speaking, however, if you prefer to ski "out of bounds" or off-piste in untracked snow, then choose a softer tele ski. I usually choose what I call a "medium" overall flex (torsionally rigid) that gives me stability in a variety of snow conditions.

On-piste lift skiers and tele racers may choose skis with a stiffer flex, especially in the tail. This will contribute to the skis' feeling of stability on packed downhill runs and provide a snappy rebound from turn to turn. Again, torsional rigidity is key.

Alpine-cambered tele skis range in weight from 5½ to 7 pounds. Tip widths of the better skis are at least 74 millimeters but tend toward the 80s—84 millimeters is considered a wide tele ski. In my opinion, the wider the better, up to about 86 millimeters, as long as they have plenty of side-cut—at least 15 to 20 millimeters' worth—and you have the right boot for that ski's width.

What's this about width? Telemark skis are getting wider; both categories described above have grown in recent years. "Fat boards," "wide rides," "widebodies"—these are all terms that have recently been added to the telemark skier's vocabulary. Many of these alpine-cambered tele skis are now widebodies. Ski width has become such a popular topic that it warrants a discussion for all types of backcountry skis.

Wide, at least on the downhills, is generally good. Wide skis have more flotation, allowing you to ride higher in crud and powder with less resistance to turning. On hardpack, wider skis give you more binding clearance and even more edge hold—*as long as you have high, stiff, supportive boots*. In general, the wider the ski, the stiffer and taller the boot you need to maintain all-around performance. That's why, with the evolution of stiffer boots, so-called "classic" telemark skis have gotten wider. Floppy boots don't provide the leverage to hold wider skis on edge, but with stiff boots wider skis are great.

Wider skis need the right technique to keep them on edge. Unlike narrow tele skis, they require more technical, angulated movements to get them up on edge.

Mounting cheap alpine skis with tele bindings has become an alternative for some telemark skiers looking for a wide ride with a skinny price tag. It's not my preference, probably in part because I design telemark skis. But honestly, I prefer the wider skis specifically designed for telemark or randonnée skiing, flexed for the free-heel skier's needs. That means lighter, snappy, torsionally rigid, and softer-flexed. The telemark turn requires weight to be more evenly distributed between skis, which means you need a softer ski to scribe the same arc.

Super-wide Skis

The third category is what I call *super-wide skis*. For difficult backcountry snow, especially when there is lots of it, I prefer short, fat randonnée skis mounted with telemark bindings. Some manufacturers are marketing these as telemark-only skis, but they were originally designed **John Falkiner** for *randonnée* skiing—the European version of ski touring. This is the

same discipline as alpine touring or ski mountaineering.

Randonnée skiers use lightweight release bindings that are hinged; the bindings can be released for uphill touring, locked down for descents. Randonnée skiers' boots are soft, hikeable plastic boots with rubber soles, very much like alpine boots. These skiers encounter the same high-mountain snow conditions as high-mountain tele skiers. They don't usually ski fast. They need skis that are light, easy-turning, and stable in difficult snow—the characteristics that make these wide boards advantageous for both tele and alpine tourers.

Randonnée skis are very wide, ranging from 88 to 92 millimeters at the tip, with lots of side-cut—at least 18 to 20 millimeters. They are generally about 10 to 20 centimeters shorter than normal length. They should have a round flex and be torsionally rigid. These aren't speed skis; they are go-anywhere skis. They feel like four-by-fours on your feet: very maneuverable at slow speeds, superb in difficult conditions.

What are the disadvantages of these new alpine/randonnée-width skis? The first is a lack of quickness edge-to-edge. A wider ski has more distance between edges, so it takes more movement—and a longer time for some skiers—to change from one edge to the other. Skiers with an alpine background may find wide skis easier because they are accustomed to those dimensions. It takes a much more precise and "angulated" skier to edge a wide ski properly, unlike a skinnier telemark ski that can be turned with minimal steering and knee movement.

Lack of speed is another disadvantage. These skis are designed specifically for easy turning in tight places. If it's speed you're after, I recommend a widebody telemark ski.

Finally, lack of kick and glide is a disadvantage. Wide skis aren't meant for general ski touring, kicking, and gliding. They're more for walking—maybe plodding—around. Kicking and gliding requires a narrower, "traditional" edged nordic ski as described above.

I often use lightweight, wide skis in the backcountry, but I climb mostly with skins, which isn't a kick-and-glide sort of situation. I do carry a can of wax for long flats, but that is to get me by; wide skis aren't designed for long flats.

Ski Length

The old-time "classic" touring ski length is measured with a ski in hand; a proper-length ski will reach from the floor to your wrist when your arm is fully upraised. Good luck turning them.

Modern, stable skis are shorter. As a rule of thumb the *longest* that you should go is height plus 25 centimeters for deep snow touring on narrower-edged nordic skis. For more focused tele downhill skiing, go height plus 20 centimeters for alpine-cambered telemark skis, and height plus about 10 centimeters for really wide boards like randonnée skis.

Other Things to Look for in Skis

Whether your skis have conventional sidewalls, angled sidewalls, or are of the newest cap or monocoque construction, their metal edges should be offset, with the edges protruding beyond the sidewall so they can be side-filed for sharpening and deburring.

The groove in the base of the ski stabilizes the ski when it is running flat. At low touring speeds the groove makes it easier to glide on one flat-running ski. When downhill racers glide on a flat ski to gain maximum speed, the groove lends stability. But grooves aren't necessary for turning. In fact, some skiers believe grooves inhibit a ski's turning ease in soft snow. Nordic-cambered skis are for kick-and-glide skiing as well as turning, so they should have a groove. With alpine-cambered tele skis, which are meant to be skied on edge most of the time, a groove isn't necessary. You'll also find that skis without a groove are much quicker to scrape after hot waxing.

Free-heel skiers' skis have a lot of force concentrated on three little mounting screws. Skis need a solid fiberglass mounting plate or wood laminate underfoot to properly hold the threads of binding screws. I recommend "tapping"—prethreading—all screw holes with a number twelve ski-service tap. This is a mandatory procedure for mounting skis with a metal topsheet. Any properly equipped alpine or nordic ski shop should be set up to do this.

If possible, you should try before you buy. Often ski shops and manufacturers offer demo programs for potential customers. It's better to pay a little more for this service than to commit your hard-earned money to a pair of mystery skis.

BOOTS

First, a rule of thumb: spend as much as you can afford on boots. If you have to compromise, do so somewhere else—sore feet equals no fun. Boots are the critical link between feet and skis.

Whether leather, plastic, or a combination of the two, backcountry boots should be comfortable for kicking steps, hiking, or "skinning" up to your favorite descent as well as perform well on the downhills. The fit should feel like that of a good hiking boot, with adequate toe room—but NOT TOO LOOSE! Boots should be snug in the instep and heel for com-

fort and control. Boots that are too loose compromise control as much as boots that are too tight compromise comfort.

Many skiers tour in their old, broken-down resort tele boots. Others have chosen softer, slightly lower versions of the new plastic boots. A number of good backcountry boots combine attributes of both plastic and leather. Leather boots' cuffs are usually fixed, so if you intend to hike in them they must be comfortable stride after stride. Leather boots should have sewn uppers with the traditional Norwegian welt. Stay away from boots with cheap injection-molded soles, which tend to fall off. Plastic boots will need a locking mechanism that allows you to free the cuff for walking and touring, and lock it back down for turning.

Boots for resort telemarking should be as laterally stiff as possible for edge control, with good fore-to-aft flexibility in the sole for telemark turning. Whether their uppers are all plastic, leather-covered plastic, or a combination of the two, boots for resort telemarking and hard-core backcountry downhill should be higher than touring models, with added stiffening. The soles of all Norwegian-welt boots need polyurethane midsoles so that they don't "noodle" too much like those built with leather or rubber midsoles. Unlike leather, plastic doesn't soften as quickly with use.

Important note: all resort/downhill-type tele boots—leather or plastic—have a very stiff forward flex when new. On the first few runs, or even the first few days, you may make great alpine turns, but your tele turns may feel like you have regressed. Be patient. These boots will break in, and your technique will adapt to the new boots' stiffness and support.

The telemarking boot's stiffer cuff should fit closely to your leg so the height and stiffness can respond to your movements. The forefoot should be snug enough to hold your foot securely. Remember, however, that you should be able to make teles by the dozens without smashing your toes. Be sure that you have enough toe room to flex forward into the tele position with little or no lift in the heel.

As telemark skiing becomes more precise, supportive footbeds are a must. Some boots come with supportive footbeds as standard equipment. There are also off-the-shelf aftermarket models that function very well. But the best footbeds are molded to your feet, designed specifically for skiers. For free-heel skiing you'll want a full-foot model footbed, rather than rear-foot only, since during the telemark turn you're putting a great deal of weight on the front part of that back foot. If you get custom footbeds for your tele boots, be sure that they can flex time after time through the telemark turn without breaking and have a forefoot material that doesn't add too much rigidity in that flexed position.

The illustrations show a heavy-duty (Norwegian-welt) backcountry   Lisa Nicholas

4
Norwegian-welt
backcountry boot

5
"Resort"
telemark boot

boot (illus. 4), a leather "resort" (downhill) telemarking boot (illus. 5), and a modern plastic boot (illus. 6).

What kind of boots do I use? I do a lot of backcountry skiing in the spring, and one of my pet peeves is soaked, noodley boots and wet feet from sloppy spring snow. New plastic boot technology eliminates all of that irritation. For both my resort and backcountry skiing I choose plastic boots with buckles, inner boots, and a lockable upper cuff that can be locked for descents or released as I walk or tour. They are warm and dry. Their design and function were inspired by randonnée boots that are used for both climbing and skiing.

Plastic or leather, the most important factors in boots are fit and comfort.

Boot Care

Plastic boots need little care, other than removing the liners for thorough drying after a hard day of skiing. Leather boots need to be waterproofed. Use a wax-based waterproofer that does not soften heel counters and toe boxes. Avoid silicone, as it may undermine the glue bond between your boots' soles and uppers. It is also a good idea to use a welt-sealing preparation. Up-and-down movements of leather nordic boots tend to pump water through the welt stitching and into your socks. To preserve their shape and comfort, store your boots on boot trees.

6
*Modern
plastic boot*

7
Supergaiters

GAITERS

Whether part of your pants or a separate accessory, gaiters should form a secure seal around your boots' uppers. Many skiers like *supergaiters* that cover the entire boot right down to the welt. The best supergaiters are those that are held securely in place by a rubber rand (see illus. 7). In cold weather they add a great deal of insulation, and in soggy spring snow, with leather boots, they are the only way to keep your feet dry from the outside. If you wear boots with buckles and pants with elasticized integral gaiters, you may not need a pair of external gaiters.

BINDINGS

Bindings are the most archaic part of the free-heel skier's kit. The newest telemark bindings still incorporate a hundred-year-old concept. Three-pin bindings offer a simple, no-nonsense attachment of boot to ski, yet they are an ancient design. The three-pin holes of a nordic boot are the Achilles' heel of the system. The marriage of those little holes and the binding's three pins is what takes all the stress of kicks, glides, turns, and head plants—and they weren't designed for that. If you use a "naked" pin binding with no reinforcement plates or cables, be sure that your boots either have a secure, molded-in metal plate that reinforces the pinholes or an exterior reinforcing plate installed properly by a boot-repair shop. Check the pinholes for erosion after each tour. It's really frustrating to set off and, miles away from the car, start kicking your ski off with every other stride or turn.

Three-pin bindings are available in many degrees of quality. Choose a strong, dependable model made from a heat-treated aluminum alloy. It should have a sturdy, riveted bail that holds your boots well back on the welt for secure boot retention and optimum ski control. It should also be adjustable for different boot-sole thicknesses.

A broken bail or ripped-out pinholes can be difficult or nearly impossible to repair with wire and duct tape. To avoid this dilemma many skiers use cable bindings for resort skiing and remote tours. They eliminate the dependence on three pins, plates, and pinholes. The cable adds more torsional rigidity to the boot for downhill control. The price you pay? You add weight and lose a bit of simplicity, but new cable bindings (illus. 8) are clean and idiot-proof.

Before leaving on your trip check to see that your cables are the right size for your boots and be sure that the cables are securely strapped together with the skis for transport. On long tours carry the appropriate adjustment wrench and a spare cable in your repair kit.

A popular option is a plate binding (illus. 9), which consists of a plastic plate that fastens under the binding and clips onto your boot heel, serving much the same purpose as the cable binding. The plate binding will preserve your boot toes and add torsional control to your boot/ski system. It also raises the binding about 1/4 inch off of the ski so that it is less likely to catch on hard snow.

Another option is a retrofit release mechanism for three-pin bindings (see illus. 10). The release is designed to reduce injuries from tips hooked on gates during races or willows off the piste. The release system definitely adds more paraphernalia and weight to your nordic downhill

8
A modern
cable binding

10
Three-pin
binding with
retrofit
releasable
binding

9
A plate
binding

system, but if safety is a priority over simplicity the releasable binding is an excellent choice.

"Stacking" bindings—raising the binding and boot off of the ski—is a relatively new practice, well proven in alpine skiing. Antivibration plates mounted under alpine bindings are common, as well as the positioning of bindings themselves much higher off of the ski. For telemark skiing this practice works very well, especially if you ski a lot of steeps on firmer snow. But it goes against traditional dogma that says that one must have the foot as close to the ski as possible. Why, then, does it work? If you have a stiff boot, it gives you more leverage on the ski by lengthening the lever arm. Most importantly, however, it raises the wings of the binding so that they (or the side of your boot) are less likely to catch and "wing out," a nasty phenomenon similar to catching a pedal on your bicycle in a tight corner. You are down before you know what happened. This phenomenon is less prevalent with wider skis, as the edge is closer to the outside of your boot.

There are stacking systems with predrilled holes and longer screws—just remove your binding, put the plates underneath, and screw the bindings back on. It's cheaper and almost as easy to put a piece of polyethylene under your skis. Unless you're racing on narrow skis, which tend to wing out badly, $1/4$ to $1/2$ inch of additional height is plenty.

POLES

Skiers use alpine and telemarking poles mainly for timing and balance. The chief purpose of nordic poles is propulsion. Backcountry poles must do it all. To be effective, poles must be of different lengths for uphill and downhill. Poles for propulsion are of the longer, classic touring length. On the downhills a shorter, alpine-length pole allows you to use the proper hand position so you don't wave your arms high in the air.

You can have your choice with adjustable poles, which can be lengthened on the uphills and flats, shortened on the downhills, and used in two different lengths for traverses. The best adjustment system that I have used is an external cam-lock arrangement that you can adjust with gloves on in brutal cold and blowing wind. Twist-lock mechanisms also work well.

Poles need comfortable, easy-to-hold grips that give good purchase to gloves and mittens. The new grips made from softer, rubbery compounds are the best. Many skiers feel that they should also have breakaway straps to help prevent shoulder injuries caused by a snagged basket. If your straps don't release, just ski without inserting your hands in them when

Lisa Nicholas,
Verbier,
Switzerland

you are in tight quarters or in the trees. Medium-sized baskets work best for most snow conditions; large ones have a heavy swing weight in the long haul and lift inordinate amounts of snow.

The most common pole-shaft material used in the backcountry is tempered aluminum. It's light, relatively inexpensive, and bends before it breaks. It lacks the notch-sensitivity of most fiberglass. There are, however, many beautiful carbon-fiber alpine poles available in alpine and adjustable varieties.

Few high-tech, fiberglass-laminate, racing-type nordic poles are robust enough for the backcountry. If you choose a fiberglass pole for skiing in the woods, buy one that is heavy duty and specially designed for serious mountain touring.

"Classic" cross-country pole length can be calculated in centimeters by multiplying your height in inches by 2.04. This is the length that is most appropriate for touring when you need to kick and glide. If you use poles of this length for telemarking, however, you'll have to hold your arms high, Harley-style.

Alpine and telemarking pole length is easily calculated as 70 percent of your height. Another way (probably the best way) to find your alpine length is to flip a pair of alpine poles upside down and then grab them right below the basket. With your elbows down, your arms should form a right angle.

SKINS

Climbing skins are used for uphill purchase. On long uphill hauls—especially with a load—skins are the best way to save energy. They give a very positive grip, and when you pull them off you have a clean pair of skis to enjoy the downhill run.

In the old days skins were made from strips of sealskin strapped to the skis with the grain of the fur pointing backward. On the forward stride, the hairs would lie down and allow the ski a little glide. When pushed back, the hairs stood up and gripped the snow.

Today most skins are made from either natural mohair or nylon plush pile. There are also plastic skins. For attachment, you can choose adhesives or numerous kinds of strap-on arrangements of metal, plastic, or nylon. I prefer adhesive. The skins are treated on the back with a reusable adhesive that can be applied, peeled off, and reapplied numerous times before being re-treated with adhesive.

In the Free-heel Ski Care chapter I describe skins and their care in depth. Also, I describe the advantages and disadvantages of the different materials and attachment systems.

To take full advantage of skins' climbability, it's a good idea to add "heel lifters" to your skis in place of standard heel plates. Inspired by randonnée bindings, these lifters (offered by several manufacturers) have a sturdy wire that can be flipped up to elevate your boot heel (see illus. 11). On long, steep climbs, this "high-heeled" position takes the stress off ankles and calf muscles, making your ski-climb more like climbing stairs.

We can talk about gear forever, but it's worthless if you don't use it. Just remember that you will never regret choosing the best gear you can afford. Ask for help from a knowledgeable friend or a trusted shop employee. Buy the kind of gear that suits you best. Then get out there and use it.

11
"Heel lifters"
for climbing

FOUNDATION
SKILLS

WEDGE TURNS

Most metal-edged skis are meant to turn. Their designs vary widely and determine how eager a ski is to turn. In general, more side-cut means more eager. Why? The waist of a side-cut ski is narrower than the tip and tail, so when it is put on its edge and weighted, it will flex into an arc. Form that arc while moving and your ski will describe a turn (see illus. 12).

The size of this turn scribed by a weighted, side-cut ski, with no other help from the skier, is too big for most terrain. To avoid slamming into things you'll have to learn how to tighten and vary your turns. Below I describe skills that add or reduce pressure on the skis, making them easier to turn. You'll learn to turn them by "steering" the skis actively with feet that are alive and moving, and you'll use the skis' edges.

Wedge turns are some of the most important turns you will learn. You'll always fall back on them, even after you've mastered telemark and parallel turns. You'll use them daily to get on lifts and to avoid other skiers or to pick your way down a corniced ridge. Ski patrollers use wedge turns to control their sleds and to get injured skiers safely down the hill. Learn them well.

Wedge turns aren't snowplow turns. They evolved from the snowplow, look similar, and many might think that they are the same. But the snowplow is an older "braking" turn—an effective one—with tips very close together and tails far apart. Wedge turns are more fluid, with more gliding, more maneuverability, and a less defensive stance. Your feet aren't static; they are moving all of the time: *alive.*

BODY POSITION

You'll need to maintain an effective athletic stance throughout all these techniques—a stable, relaxed, in-balance position that frees your body to act and react quickly and easily. Try it: relax your back muscles and "cup" your upper body, pulling your navel in toward your backbone. Feel your weight centered on both feet.

The stability test: assume the stance I've described. Rock back and

Pages 44–45:
Team Clambin
in Kasmir

12
The arc
described by
a side-cut ski

forth from your toes to your heels. Now try it the wrong way: arch your back, tense it, and rock back and forth. Which way feels more balanced? Which way would you catch a basketball? There's no substitute for a round, relaxed back.

I always use this athletic stance. I think especially hard about it whenever the skiing is difficult. It keeps my back from hurting. It's a familiar focus to rely on, one that always works. When I lose my balance to the rear, this stance helps me get out of a desperate position—the "back seat." It "collects" my body into a stable, strong position.

GETTING STARTED

Let's get on snow. Put your skis on in a flat spot where you can practice a few exercises. First, lift one foot, then the other. Get the feel of having skis on your feet. Raise your toes, then point them down. Standing on one foot, point your ski tip to the right, then to the left. Change feet and do the same.

Now, from a solid stance on both feet, hop your ski tails into a wedge. Your toes should be pointed inward, your hips, shoulders, and head centered between the skis. Your ski tips should be several inches apart. This is a wedge position.

THE STRAIGHT RUN

Here's a term that might be new to you: *fall line.* The fall line is the direction a ball would roll when tossed down a slope. It's gravity's choice, the most direct downhill-sloping path. Some call it the "fun line." Find a very gentle slope, ski-packed or groomed, with a good runout. Pick an obstacle-free fall line on your slope. Start with the correct body position, your athletic stance: stomach in, back round and relaxed, ankles flexed with knees forward. Keep your eyes on the road ahead—not at your ski tips.

Point your skis down the hill and ready . . . Go! Push off with your poles for momentum. Skis should be parallel at about hip width (see top figure in illus. 13). Let your skis run straight to the bottom. Keep your ankles and knees flexed and relaxed. Keep your weight centered on your feet, both side-to-side and fore-to-aft.

If that was too easy, we'll make it more interesting. Take another straight run, but this time, shuffle your feet back and forth without lifting your heels. Try standing on one foot, then another. Hop up and down. Go back to a shuffle. You want to feel as though your feet are mobile, flexible, loose, not stuck in a static position. That's what I mean by feet that are *alive.*

13
*Straight run
to a wedge*

THE WEDGE

Try it again, but this time, gently push your heels out, keeping your toes pointed inward. Don't worry about using your edges; stay light on them. It should feel as though you are *brushing* the skis out into a wedge, not grinding them. Let your skis glide as you brush them out, pushing your heels away from you. Are they in a wedge? Now widen your wedge by pushing on your heels; see if you can brake to a stop (see illus. 13).

Experiment with the width of your wedge. See what happens when you brush your ski tails farther apart, then let them glide closer together.

It's important when using a wedge not to lock your knees together. Keep them apart, as though you were riding a horse or holding a soccer ball or even a basketball between them. Do the same with your ski tips: keep them apart, almost a soccer ball's width. If your tips want to cross, begin your wedge with your feet farther apart, at hip width.

To slow down, push out on your heels and widen the wedge. This is the "braking" wedge: as your feet widen, your skis tip over more onto their edges. This "edging" puts on the brakes.

Use this wedge width to vary the braking action—wider for more braking, narrower for less. Just take care to avoid locked knees when you put on the brakes.

Flex your ankles, pressing on the inside edges. Don't roll your ankles inward: just flex them, pressing on those edges. Now vary the wedge: go back and forth from a narrow wedge with more glide to a wide wedge with more edge and braking action. Feel your speed change as increased edging slows you down, decreased edging speeds you up. Imagine that a tree just appeared in front of you and make an emergency stop. Note: if you are having trouble slowing yourself to a stop, tighten your boots. Think of pressure building under the big-toe sides of both feet.

DOING A WEDGE TURN

Let's try a turn. Let your skis run to get some momentum and then sink into a wedge—this time a narrow one to keep your speed. Next, exaggerate the wedging movement with one foot; press harder on one foot as you wedge it. Think of squashing a bug under the ball of your foot. You will turn in the direction that your squashing foot is pointing. That means that squashing with your right foot turns you left. Squashing with the left foot turns you right (see illus. 14).

14
A wedge turn

15
Linked
wedge turns

From now on, in all of your turns, I'll refer to this squashing foot—the turning foot (and ski)—as the *outside foot* (and ski). It's called that because it is on the outside of your turn's arc. You will also hear this foot called the *downhill* foot—it is on the downhill side of the turn. In the illustration, the skier's squashing foot is highlighted.

To link your turns, gather some speed and alternate your squashing feet. Make shallow little arcs. Turn only with your feet, not with your upper body. Alternate squashing feet, shifting pressure from one foot to another. Be sure to keep your ankles and knees flexed and relaxed. Make some snaky S curves down the hill. Try controlling your speed with repeated turns. Get up some steam at the top; then try to slow down by turning in a narrow, gliding wedge. Even when you use less edging, turning out of the fall line will slow you down (see illus. 15).

Now make another run and widen your wedge, controlling your speed with your edges. Feel how the edges control your speed?

Next try moving up and down. Rise up between turns and squash down on that foot to turn. Rise up and squash down, up, down.

Once you've got it, practice so that it sinks in. Vary your wedge width and turn size. Make a few wide turns, a few narrow ones, then wide ones again. With these skills you are using the braking wedge, the gliding wedge, and the wedge turn.

BASIC TELEMARK

Sondre Norheim, the father of the telemark, first used his telemark as a stable landing position after a long jump. Who knows? Maybe Norheim felt himself yanked forward landing an 80-meter jump and instinctively made a telemark as a survival measure to avoid a nasty face-plant. However it happened, Norheim's landing stance gave him fore-to-aft stability.

My first experience telemarking was in 1971, in the little town ski area north of Gunnison, Colorado. I don't remember much about it, just some confusion about which foot went forward when turning. I do remember my skis, a narrow pair of wooden Splitkeins.

My next memory is more vivid. It was a few days later, in Crested Butte. The day was perfect, warm and sunny on Snodgrass Mountain. There were 5 or 6 inches of light snow on a firm base.

I picked a nice-looking slope, waxed my skis, and packed a good climbing track up the hill. By then I had figured out which foot to put forward, but the first couple of times that I stuck out a lead ski not much happened—just huge arcs to a stop. Then it worked. I turned my front foot a little more with the turn and made my first telemark. What a feeling! I could only turn one way, though, so my next goal was to copy my movements in the other direction.

Why had I chosen to learn telemark? I had a dream of doing everything—uphill and downhill, backcountry and piste—on one kind of ski.

You don't have to be a jumper—or a dreamer—to appreciate the tele. It's a great choice in cruddy snow, very deep powder, or any conditions that yank your feet back while throwing your body forward. The telemark's genuflecting position has superior fore-to-aft stability. It braces the skier to help prevent uncomfortable forward falls.

It is easiest to learn telemarks, or any ski turn for that matter, through a logical learning progression. The following section is a skill progression to teach you a variety of necessary moves: the telemark position, the lead change, the shuffle or half-wedge turn, and the basic tele turn. If you take enough time with each skill they will all work like building blocks toward your goal.

I'm going to give you some options for learning the basic telemark

Australian telemarks in Verbier

54

from a striding position or a half-wedge position. Try both and plug in to the one that works best for you. I've tried to be spare with the language. You will learn much better if you have a brief explanation of what to do, feel it and discover for yourself, and then study tips for improvement as you progress and develop your own questions.

THE TELEMARK STANCE

Your body position is fundamental. Start on a flat spot with the telemark stance, using your athletic body position: a round, relaxed back and a cupped stomach. Sink into a tele. Sink straight down, sliding one foot forward and one foot back. *Your weight should stay evenly distributed between both feet.* Experiment with a very tall stance and a very low stance, and find a comfortable spot in the middle. You should feel your weight resting on your whole front foot and on the ball of your rear foot (see illus. 16).

16
The telemark
stance

LEARNING THE TELEMARK
FROM A STRIDING POSITION

Learning the telemark from a striding position is a method that has withstood the test of time. It originated from a *diagonal stride,* the classic cross-country stride. But even if you have heard of this before, please pay attention to the one way that my explanation differs from this walking/ skiing stride: arms. This is important: stride with your feet, *not* with your arms. Don't swing your arms as you do in a cross-country stride. Simply keep them relaxed and a bit in front of you (see illus. 17).

In the flats, stride from one telemark position to another, taking exaggerated, bent-legged strides. Move as though you're trying to stay low and invisible in tall grass. It should be as much a sense of dropping down as it is of striding forward. You should be getting a good quad workout.

OK, now the hill. You'll need a good practice slope. The best practice terrain is a ski-area beginner's slope that is well packed and groomed. If you are lucky the slope will have a slow-moving lift. If a lift is not available, find a gentle slope with a flat, obstacle-free runout. Pack the loose snow by side-stepping up and down the slope.

Pick a very gentle downhill that you can straight run without fear. Point your skis straight down the slope, push off, and make those same striding moves straight down the hill. Terrain selection is important for this exercise; the goal here is a *slow* downhill on a *slight* incline that allows you to run straight with your skis flat.

Time out for a couple of new terms. First, *steering*. Steering is physically turning your ski—I call it "pointing" the ski with your foot. If you didn't already learn it in the section on wedge turns, the second term you need to know is *fall line*. It's the line a ball would take if you rolled it down a hill. When skiers say "step into the fall line," or "face down the fall line," they mean "step directly down the hill," or "face down the hill."

Now you're ready to try a telemark turn. At the same time that you stride into a new telemark position, steer (twist) your front foot into a turn. Remember that, just as in the wedge, the foot that you're pointing is the *outside* foot, and you're pointing it to the *inside* of the turn. Try turns one at a time, on each side. Turn your skis across the hill until you come to a stop. As you progress, think not only of your foot, but point your ski, foot, and knee into the turn (see illus. 17).

As you gain confidence, on your easiest slope, start striding from turn to turn. Make your turns smaller, using the striding motion practiced above, steering each forward foot (and ski and knee) inside the turn.

*17
Striding into a
telemark*

Once you get your balance, you'll find yourself striding from little tele to little tele, making S curves. Your front foot will feel more active as you stride, but don't forget your rear foot. Stride into each tele with fifty-fifty weight distribution.

LEARNING THE TELEMARK
FROM A HALF-WEDGE

This is another option for learning the basics. My first exposure to the half-wedge approach was through my PSIA Nordic Demonstration Team coach. The coach, a longtime downhill instructor, showed me how this alpine-style idea was likely to avert the classic bad habits that plague the neophyte telemarker.

Begin with a straight run on your practice slope. Point one ski straight and wedge the other ski out (see illus. 18).

18
The half wedge
(on either side)

A note about weight: don't weight the wedged ski too much; you should feel its edge lightly brush against the snow. Your weight should remain focused on the straight-running ski. You'll find that although your weight is on your straight-running ski, the pressure that develops on the wedged ski initiates a direction change. To make turns, press harder against the wedged ski. Try these little turns on either side, keeping most of the weight on the straight-running ski but pressing against that wedged one.

OK, time out for more terms. From now on I'll refer to the straight-running ski as your *inside* ski, since it's the ski on the inside once you make a turn. The wedged ski I'll call the *outside* ski—it's the turning ski on the outside of the arc.

Make S curves, rhythmically linking shallow half-wedge turns (see illus. 19). Your weight will shift as your inside ski changes to your outside ski; as your weight moves to the new inside ski, the outside ski's edge brushes the snow and pulls you into a turn. You'll have the sensation that your legs are swinging back and forth under your body.

The transition from half-wedges to telemarks is the next step. Begin making half-wedge turns. As you wedge the outside ski slide it forward and sink into the telemark stance. (Some skiers prefer to think of sliding the *inside* ski back rather than the outside ski forward. Try it and see which works for you.)

As you sink into that telemark stance, steer (point) the advanced front ski through a turn. Practice one turn at a time, beginning in a traverse and turning uphill to a stop. (What's a *traverse?* A traverse is gliding across the hill using your uphill edges to maintain a horizontal course.) Sink *between* your feet, with both skis equally weighted. Practice this "stop-turn" in both directions.

GARLANDS

Using either the striding-to-tele approach or the half-wedge-to-tele, once you become more comfortable turning to a stop in each direction you are ready to practice a *garland*. The exercise is named for the pattern your skis scribe in the snow. It's done by executing a series of stop-turns, progressively beginning each turn more in the fall line. It's a very useful way to develop confidence in your turns.

Start by picking a shallow, traversing line and turn uphill to a stop. As your confidence grows, step into the fall line a little more each time you

19
Shallow half-
wedge turns

begin a new stop-turn. Each turn starts with less traverse until finally there is no traverse at all. Once you are comfortable turning without a traverse, step directly down the hill, beginning the stop-turn *in the fall line* (see illus. 20).

LINKING TURNS

On the easier part of your slope, try linking some stride- or wedge-teles down the hill. Sink into the telemark position at the same time you steer that front foot, knee, and ski. On a gentle slope you will feel as though you are walking "pigeon-toed" from one tele to the next. Steer your front foot more to make a tighter turn and slow down, steer less to speed up.

20
A half wedge into a tele-garland

MOTION

With practice you will find yourself thinking less of strides or half-wedges and more of a tele-to-tele movement. You'll pick up this sensation more quickly if you practice on very moderate slopes. As the slope steepens, you'll need to tele-turn your skis across the hill to check your speed. Then the transition to the next turn becomes more defined, a determined move into each successive telemark. To ease this transition and make each upcoming turn effective, you'll need to amplify what skiers simply call *motion* or *movement*. Remember my earlier reference to feet that are *alive*? This is the next step—motion that brings your *whole body* alive to smoothly get those skis around.

This movement is the key to linking your turns smoothly. Simplified, you could call it "up-and-down" movement. But it's not really that simple. It's dynamic movement—up, down, forward, and back; never static; never in a "position."

The purpose is to use your body's entire range of motion. Try it: stand tall at the beginning of your turn—much taller than in the classic telemark position you first practiced. Then sink through each tele turn as you make your arc, finishing the turn in that "classic" stance. Exaggerate tall and small. Stand up tall for the next turn and repeat the sinking motion through the arc.

As you sink, steer and edge your front ski. Each time you initiate a new turn, stand up again, sink, and steer. Your weight should be on the inside (uphill) edges of both skis. Feel the difference that the motion makes? Soon you'll be gracefully linking telemark turns one after another.

BASIC PARALLEL TURNS

I love parallel turns. Some of my buddies say that I'm cheating. There is no such thing as cheating. Anyway, if they could do them they'd probably cheat, too.

Parallel turns work. They are stable and efficient. They are remarkable on the steeps. Learn them to be an all-around skier.

One ski season years ago, I set a goal to improve my free-heel parallel turns. I skied as much as possible with alpine skiers, watching and mimicking them. I began to use parallel turns in more varied conditions. First I practiced parallels only on hard snow, where the skis were easy to steer. I made the most of the technique's stable side-to-side stance. As my turns became stronger I mixed them up, using them where least appropriate, trying to strengthen my parallel turns in powder and crud. Of course, I augured a lot, but I kept working at it. By the end of the season my parallels were coming around.

Why parallel? When terrain is steep, icy, or the space very tight for turning, parallel and other alpine techniques work great. The parallel's compact stance allows quick and efficient direction changes. Parallels are deceptively quick turns—and they are elegant.

Teles and parallels aren't all there is. To be a versatile, go-anywhere skier on all kinds of equipment you'll need to master a variety of maneuvers: wedges, wedge christies, stem christies, and parallels. Approached one by one, these moves form an ideal learning progression for developing the necessary foundation for strong, advanced parallel turns.

WEDGE AND STEM CHRISTIES

John Falkiner,
Chamonix

After wedge turns, *wedge christies* and *stem christies* are two of the skills that will build your foundation for strong parallel turns. Stem christies are often used at this stage for skiers who must learn on more difficult terrain and in ungroomed snow. The stem christy is initiated with one ski actively *stemmed* (wedged) out into a V—almost stepped into the V. The turn is finished with the skis "matched," or parallel. The parallel skid that finishes the turn is called a *christy*.

Wedge christies move both skis together. In both turns, your skis move from wedge to parallel position. A culinary image you can keep in mind is "pizza (wedge or stem), fries (two parallel french fries), pizza, fries, pizza, fries." In working toward parallel, I'd recommend practicing both, starting first with wedge christies.

DOING A WEDGE CHRISTY

Make some short-radius wedge turns in the fall line. Be sure that your ski tips aren't too close together. Like your knees, your ski tips should have almost a soccer ball's width between them. A smaller-sized wedge—less of a V-shape—works best for these shorter turns.

Work on the shape of your wedge turn. You'll need a bit more speed. Think about making very *round* turns instead of shallower S-shaped turns. Steer that outside foot, knee, and ski into the new turn. You need the speed because round turns slow you down—round turns are great for controlling speed on steeper slopes.

Feel your edges? Most likely you will be using your edges more, both to control and to use the speed to shape those round turns.

Keep up the round turns, steering that outside ski. Once that's comfortable, think of your *inside* ski: *lighten your inside ski through the turn.* That's right, *lighten* that inside ski. Don't lift it, just lighten it. What happened? Did it slide alongside your outside ski? Right on! That's a wedge christy! (See illus. 21).

Some skiers prefer to think of transferring weight to the outside ski rather than lightening the inside one. Try both, and do what works best for you.

DOING A STEM CHRISTY

I remember watching three of Hans Gmoser's helicopter guides descending from the summit plateau of Mount Logan, the highest peak in Canada's Yukon. They were skiing roped together. I watched carefully in hopes of gleaning some off-piste alpine tricks that I could use for our free-heeled descent. To my surprise they were all making controlled stem christies. No parallels, even in the easier snow! Teles sufficed to get us down, but I wanted to know more about using the stem christy in these situations.

If you must control your speed for dicey skiing, the stem christy is an excellent turn. Advanced skiers use it because the stem produces a quick, controlled-turn initiation, a key to avoiding the sudden acceleration

21
A wedge
christy

present in the first half of a parallel turn. Stem christies provide excellent side-to-side stability, an indispensable element for negotiating crevasses—especially with a big pack.

As I mentioned earlier, the word *christy* defines a parallel skid with both skis edged in the same direction. Stem christies have a stemmed-turn initiation with a weight shift to the outside ski, resulting in a skidded christy or parallel finish.

Try it. From a traverse, stand up tall and stem your outside ski into a wedge position. Stand up as though you want to reach out with that stemming ski. Then *step onto it,* shifting your weight to the stemmed ski.

Steer your ski into the fall line. Sink with your body as you steer through the turn, preparing to stand up for the next stem. Now stem the other ski and *step onto it*. I call this move a *stem-step*. Shift your weight to that stemmed ski. Both skis are then steered parallel into the christy turn finish.

Practice first in a garland, turning only in one direction from a traverse. Unlike when you did your first teles, there's no need to step-turn into the fall line. Let your stem bring you around. Stand up tall and stem-step, then sink and steer your turn around to a stop. Feel the flowing sensation that standing up and sinking produce as you swoop through the fall line.

The next step, linking stem christies, feels quite natural: once you steer your last turn across the fall line, stand tall and stem-step your new outside ski, shifting your weight onto it. With your weight shifted, you're now steering into your next turn (see illus. 22).

Stand up, sink, stand up, sink—this is an important movement that I will emphasize time and time again throughout this book. It's an

22
Linked stem christies

unweighting—the sinking lightens your skis. If you don't believe me, try it on your bathroom scale. Stand tall and sink abruptly. Notice how your weight drops when you sink down. Your skis stay lighter, easier to steer, as long as you are sinking.

Here's another exercise: lighten your inside ski as you steer both skis through the fall line. Think "light as a feather" on the inside ski. This gets you steering and turning your outside ski. Your light inside ski will drift parallel to "match" the outside ski—forming that stable parallel christy in your turn finish. Some skiers actually lift their inside ski when they stem-step to exaggerate this lightness (see the last figure in illus. 22).

Now review the three points of focus that will make wedge and stem christies much easier: (1) use plenty of up-and-down movement, starting tall and sinking through the turn; (2) shift your weight onto that stemmed (or wedged) ski; and (3) lighten the inside ski as your skis come through the fall line.

STEERING

By lightening your inside ski in the last exercise you've probably already made some basic parallel turns. The next thing to think about is *steering*.

As you make wedge or stem christies, think of *steering* your inside ski: turn it with your inside foot in the direction of the new turn. That's right. As you lighten your inside ski, actively steer it alongside the outside ski. Move onto the new outside ski, lighten and steer the inside one. Using whichever focal point for steering that best suits your preference, think of pointing your ski, foot, or knee in the direction that you want to go. Are your feet moving together, steering and open-stance parallel?

Try it again. Start with smooth, round, linked stem or wedge christies. Feel the inside ski lighten as you transfer your weight to your outside foot and steer it. Steer the inside foot along with it. You don't need to lift it; as the inside foot lightens, it's easy to steer alongside the outside one (see illus. 23).

MOTION

Now, forget your feet for a minute. Think about *motion:* standing very tall at the start of the turn as you steer your feet into the fall line, then sinking deeply with your ankles and your knees through the turn. Exaggerate this extension (tall) and flexion (small) so your skis feel light and

23
A basic
parallel
turn . . .
tall, small

maneuverable as you start each new turn. Tall, small, tall, small.

Inhale deeply when you stand up and start your turn; exhale as you sink through the turn. Inflate to be tall; exhale to be small. Get the feel for this kind of vertical motion and you'll have a fundamental skill that will be with you no matter what technique you choose.

Let's take a break from turning for a minute to practice a few critical skills that are important techniques in themselves and that will help your parallel skiing.

SIDE-SLIPPING

Side-slipping is controlled skidding—releasing your edges and flattening your skis to slide sideways down the hill. Side-slipping isn't just for skill development; it's a technique. Sure, it's an important basic; but a good side-slip is crucial to pressure control in the most advanced skiing. On something steep and narrow I find that, snow allowing, a short side-slip is just what it takes to gain momentum for that difficult first turn.

Practice your side-slip on a short, steep, packed slope. Note: first, take time to tighten your boots. I've often had students who didn't want to hassle with tightening their boots, and they have sacrificed ski and edge control.

Begin by climbing up from the bottom, side-stepping to the top. Are your skis slipping out from under you? If so, then tip them into the hill a little more. Don't lean; just tip the skis, edging with your feet, ankles, and (to a lesser degree) your knees. Once you are partway up the slope, try a downhill side-slip. Face your body downhill: round, relaxed back; stomach in; head up. Then, with your skis *across the fall line,* let up on your edges, rolling your feet and knees away from the hill. Your skis should side-slip down the hill.

Develop control of your side-slip by alternately flattening your skis and edging them to come to a halt. Try to slide sideways only, with a minimum of forward motion (see illus. 24).

24
Side-slipping

Now try a forward side-slip. This time forward motion is OK. Start in a slightly downhill traverse. Rise up and roll your knees *away* from the hill and let your skis side-slip; now sink and roll them *into* the hill so that they grip and your skis hold the traverse. Experiment with the amount of side-slip so that your skis grip, then slide, then grip, making a wobbly path across the hill.

HERRINGBONE

Herringbone is an alternative climbing technique to the side-step that you practiced in the last exercise. It's what I would call a "short-term climbing technique"—something that you will use for short distances. Because of its foot-splayed position, it's used in place of the side-step on gentler slopes. It is, essentially, walking duck-footed up the hill (see illus. 25).

25
Herringbone

Make a wedge, backwards: with your tips spread, tails together, step uphill from inside edge to inside edge. Press the insides of your feet into the hill to gain more edge. Try it with less edge, then more edge, to get a feel of how much edge it requires to grip on your slope.

A SET OF GARLANDS

The last two exercises focused on edge control. Now we'll build on those exercises and try a set of garlands. We'll make a series of parallel stop-turns, progressively beginning each turn more in the fall line.

Start by picking a shallow traversing line and turn uphill to a stop. Weight and steer your outside ski away from the fall line, and at the same time, *lighten and steer the inside one.* Feel the skis "match," parallel?

As your confidence grows, step into the fall line a little more each time you begin a new stop-turn. Each turn starts with less traverse, until finally there is no traverse at all. Once you are comfortable turning without a traverse, step directly down the hill, beginning the stop-turn in the fall line. Don't forget the vertical motion. Sometimes I think of this movement as "sink and steer, rise, sink and steer."

A note about your feet: be sure to keep them hip width—no narrower (refer back to illus. 23). Don't worry if you feel a bit wobbly. With practice you will soon feel more solid. Practicing hockey stops (the next exercise) will help solidify your two-footed steering—steering not only your weighted outside foot into the turn, but your lighter inside foot in the same direction. Hockey stops are a very abrupt version of a parallel turn with lots of skid. As you temper, or soften, those abrupt movements, your parallels will get more carvy and elegant.

HOCKEY STOPS

You need a good emergency stop. The *hockey stop* is the quintessential slamming on the brakes. Learn it well.

A hockey stop isn't just for stopping. Practice it and you'll develop greater maneuverability and control for your parallel turns. Its abrupt two-footed steering/twisting and resultant two-footed skid are just over-exaggerated versions of the two-footed steering and christy of the basic parallel turn.

Work on hockey stops on a smooth slope. Standing tall, point your skis straight down the hill in a wide, stable stance. Push off for speed. Once you gain momentum, sink abruptly, flexing at the ankles and knees (not at the waist!) and steer (twist) your skis *hard* across the fall line.

26
A hockey
stop

Continue facing down the hill as your skis come across the slope. Your parallel skis will skid you to a stop (see illus. 26).

Do lots of hockey stops in both directions so that you are comfortable stopping on either side. Remember, this is your emergency stop. One note of warning: practice it *below* obstacles—or your friends—to avoid dangerous collisions. I've seen too many skiers try to stop above a group of waiting friends and instead wipe them all out.

FLEXION AND EXTENSION

When I refer to up-and-down movement, or vertical motion, I often put the phrase in quotes. That's because flexion and extension of your legs really doesn't create a purely up-and-down motion. I'm not trying to get you popping straight up and down like toast out of the toaster. Rather, the angle of the hill makes the movement of your body fall somewhere between up-and-down and in-and-out. It's an overall flexion and extension motion of your body. I can't emphasize this motion too much.

Try making some turns with lots of flexion and extension—tall, small, tall, small. Then make some turns with no movement at all. Which do you prefer? In all downhill techniques, flexion and extension movements are what make the skis work for you. They allow you to control and use the pressures that gravity and centrifugal force create against your edges. They are the key to more carve and less skid (refer back to illus. 22, 23).

There are many more tips in the Advanced Skills section devoted specifically to these kinds of movements. The point is to develop a *three-dimensional* motion in your skiing—a flowing down the hill while your body moves dynamically into the fall line, extending and flexing, in and out. Stick with it. Move all of the time. Stay away from "positions"; be *alive* as you ski.

John Falkiner on the Haute Route, Switzerland

The Haute Route

We barely bridged the icy glacial stream, popped off our skis, and stumbled up the moraine. Up a steep incline was a closed ski trail covered in ice, year-old cow shit, and pine cones. Perfect. We might not have to walk. This icy minefield dropped us in the village of Furi. An open outdoor stube shimmered like a mirage, an oasis. Behind it was the téleferique that dropped steeply to Zermatt.

Beer, beautiful beer.

We dumped our packs on the grass and ordered a round. Richard looked awful, but he was OK. His face was covered with dried blood. He had taken a nasty twisting fall in the difficult snow of the lower Tiefmatten glacier. In the wet, heavy, abrasive mank he had carved a turn with the bridge of his nose. It wasn't all like that; off the top of the Col de Valpelline—our last pass—we had carved what seemed like endless tight turns on perfect corn.

My French friends and I were giddy, sipping pressions from huge steins; tired, elated, and crinkly from sun and sweat. Our conversation was comical. My Italian companion had bailed in Arolla with sore feet and would meet us in Zermatt for the Monte Rosa. Without Marco's pigeon French, our communication *was reduced to my speaking slowly in Italian and waving my arms, my friends replying slowly in French and waving their arms, and all of us wondering if Romance languages were really so similar.*

That was an excerpt from the diary that I kept on the Haute Route. Chamonix-Zermatt-Saas Fee makes up the Haute Route, the best-known ski mountaineering route in Europe. Its setting is breathtaking and, in spite of today's touristy popularity, it is *the* Haute Route—the first established high ski traverse through the Alps and still considered one of the best lines. Compared with other routes, the Haute Route is crowded, with mediocre huts and pathetic Swiss and French beer. Still, it's classic—even though there are numerous longer, more remote routes closer to Bavarian taps.

This "classic" Haute Route (there are numerous variants) evolved with the early exploration of its individual high peaks and passes in the Swiss and French Alps. The peaks and passes were linked together in 1861 by a French-guided group of British, who named it the High-level Road—translated into French as Haute Route. It might seem strange that this famous route was pioneered by the Brits, but they were some of the keenest pioneers of skiing and general alpine exploration. In traditional European style, they hired local guides as part of their party. It's thought that, as late as the mid-1950s, no unguided British parties had completed the Haute Route.

Today the Haute Route passes through a number of modern alpine resorts. Although they find it a far cry from resort skiing, tourers make use of lifts and *téleferiques* (cable cars) to get to snowline, avoiding unnecessary climbs and adding to the downhill skiing. One can get used to that custom very quickly.

The skiing on the Haute Route, unless you take certain detours, need not be difficult. I remember one friend who briefed me for the trip saying that the skiing was dead-easy: "With a strong snowplow and controlled side-slip you could do the route." In retrospect, I would agree that you could *do* it, but it would be a shame to miss some of the exciting detours and smooth, steep, beautiful corn slopes. And, if all you had was a wedge and a side-slip in your repertoire, you'd probably find yourself scared stiff wedging down some exposed arête with a village at your feet—thousands of feet below.

This style of skiing, when compared with normal piste and off-piste lift skiing, is like alpine climbing as compared with sport climbing: ski mountaineering requires many skills beyond the perfect turn. In fact, you don't need the perfect turn. It's more important to have survival skiing skills in all conditions.

Skiing in Europe is different. If it's wilderness that you are after, Europe isn't the place to tour. It's expensive; téleferiques are often visible from remote places; routes can be crowded; and huts prevail. But given the mountains, the incredible hut systems, and the support of an established ski mountaineering "culture," it's easy to take the disadvantages in stride. Any skier who has stood on top of one of the big peaks like the Jungfrau, the Monte Rosa, or Mont Blanc is already planning the next trip.

MAINTENANCE

FREE-HEEL SKI CARE

Your approach to ski care depends on how much time, effort, and money you're willing to invest. You can spend hours on the rituals of waxing and tuning, or you can keep the waxing simple and have someone else do the tuning. Either way, caring for your skis properly can make a big difference in their performance.

WAXING YOUR SKIS

In the wax room the night before a cross-country race it might seem so, but waxing isn't alchemy. It can be as simple or as complex an art as you choose to make it. For backcountry use, keep it simple. You may have a suitcase of wax at home, but what you take to the wilderness should fit into the palm of your hand. Not only will you save weight but decisions about the wax will be much simpler.

Most wax manufacturers offer a two-wax system—one wax for wet snow and one for dry—and a color-coded system organized according to temperature. My wilderness wax kit includes a can of two-wax system "wet" for kick in wetter snow, a couple of colder waxes (a blue and a purple) for kick in dryer snow, a little piece of universal glide wax, and green for glider and super-cold kick. In spring I add a universal *klister* for very abrasive, refrozen snow. Combine this ultralight wax kit with a pair of stick-on skins for long, steeper climbs, and you can go just about anywhere.

A Little Alchemy

The right cross-country kick wax *does* work like magic. It grips the snow—or, in fact, the snow grips it—by "crystalline bonding." All this means is that when the ski is weighted, the snow crystals stick into the wax, giving you purchase. Colder, dryer snow crystals are sharper and better defined. Colder waxes are harder because these sharper crystals have greater "grip." Warmer crystals are more rounded—and wetter—so the wax must be softer for the crystals to grip. Refrozen crystals are not only round and wet, but abrasive, so klister must be softer and very abrasion resistant—long-lasting on your skis (and gloves and pants).

Glide wax is a harder wax of a different chemistry that is not meant to grip but to glide. It nourishes skis' polyethylene bases and makes them glide and turn more easily. It is also temperature-matched for the highest performance and is usually applied with a hot iron and then scraped to a thin film. It's important to glide-wax your skis as often as possible. In the backcountry, it's sufficient to rub on a little universal glide wax.

A Simplified Kick-waxing System

In the backcountry I use what I call a "modified two-wax system" for kick wax, using the "wet" wax from the two-wax system plus a few harder kick waxes for dryer snow. I'll take silver (from the two-wax system) for wet snow; and for dry snow, extra blue, extra purple, and extra green (from the color-coded system). Some of the newest waxes go by other designations, like "VF 40," "VF 30," "VF 20," and so on, instead of colors. The cans, though, are still color-coded. The newer waxes are expensive, but ice less and grip better than the older waxes. For me they're worth the extra cost. It's easy once you get past the techie names. Just refer to the manufacturer's color-coded cans. (For simplicity in the following discussion, I'll use colors instead of the techie names.)

At the trailhead, make a snowball. If the snow is wet enough to pack into a good, moist ball—a real window-breaker—use silver. If the snow is too dry to pack, go to the dryer waxes. Among the dryer waxes, when the temperature is close to freezing, use the purple; if it's clear and cold—but not bitter cold—go blue; and if it's bitter cold, green.

"Crayon" your chosen wax on the ski in the "kick zone." For colder waxes like blue or green, you can wax the full length of the ski. In fact, I often apply blue or green full length as a base coat. For softer, warmer waxes, it's best to be conservative. I'd wax the middle three-fourths of the ski for purple, and the middle couple of feet for the wet silver.

Once your skis are waxed start up the trail and test your wax job. If it works, don't fix it. If a ski slips, lengthen the "kicker" toward the tip and tail, or add another layer if you waxed full length. If it still slips, add more layers, smoothing each one with a cork. Several smooth, thin layers are more effective than one thick one. And if it still slips, switch to a softer wax, starting with a smooth, thin layer again. As you go softer, start shorter, waxing the middle of the ski first (2 to 3 feet) and then lengthening the kick if you continue to slip.

Klister

As I said earlier, the penetration ability of snow (the sharpness of its crystals) into hard wax is a function of temperature and water content.

Warmer and wetter snow requires a softer wax, which the rounded, moisture-laden snow grains can penetrate. Klister is used as a kick wax for old, refrozen snow, snow so abrasive that it necessitates a more durable, sticky wax. Klister is just as durable on your clothes as on your skis, so be careful with both the tube and the waxed skis. A zip-lock bag for unused klister is mandatory.

Klister must be applied warm—otherwise it's too difficult to get out of the tube's little orifice. If it's cold, you'll more than likely squeeze the tube too hard and get klister oozing unexpectedly from the back side of the tube. That's a bummer. To prevent tube blowout, warm the tube carefully over a torch or your cook stove, or carry it (in a plastic bag) inside your jacket.

Once the warmed klister is viscous, apply a short, sparing bead to the wax pocket of the ski (about 12 to 18 inches from the heel forward). Then smooth it with a klister spatula or putty knife. Use it sparingly; less is best. If it's difficult to smooth, carefully apply a little heat to the wax with a torch or stove. I sometimes use the heel of my hand to smooth klister. Don't worry about getting it on your hands; just put your gloves back on and deal with it later.

"Now try taking klister off," you say. I've awakened to new snow on many spring skiing trips after having applied copious amounts of klister the previous day. Armed with only a putty knife I've been able to remove almost all traces of the sticky wax. The trick is the temperature. I cool the skis in the shade, then run the putty knife lengthwise along each ski, sliding the blade under the klister next to the base and peeling it off. The clean ski is then ready for cold wax and fresh snow.

Glide Wax

Rounding out my backcountry system is a chunk of universal glider. Glide wax nourishes and protects a polyethylene base, preventing it from hardening and oxidizing. It protects skis when traveling. I leave a heavy coat on my skis for the trip and scrape it down once I arrive at my destination. Glide wax also makes skiing easier. Not only are the skis faster up the trail but they turn more readily. Almost all turns are partly skidded, and glide wax makes the skid much easier.

For touring, gliders should be applied only to the tip and tail of a ski. If applied under the foot they can inhibit the adhesion of the kick wax. If skis are used for downhill only, or just with skins, the entire base should be waxed. At home that's best done with a dry (not steam) iron set on medium heat. Hold the wax against the iron and drip it onto the ski. (If

**Ace Kvale
waxin' up**

the wax smokes, the iron is too hot.) Then iron the wax into the ski, being sure to keep the iron moving to prevent damage to the base of the ski. After the wax has cooled, scrape it with a sharp plastic scraper. In cold temperatures the wax should be almost invisible. For warm conditions the wax can be a little thicker, but it should still be scraped thoroughly.

In the backcountry you can rub glider on a ski like kick wax and then cork it smooth. This method is not as durable as ironing but is quite effective when an outlet isn't available. I also use universal alpine glider paste in a tube. It can be rubbed on and polished with a handkerchief.

Wax Choices

If you want to experiment with different colors of kick wax, stick with one brand until its use is second nature. Then, if you continue to experiment, try the most popular colors in other brands. Choose a wax color by matching the temperature with the wax's temperature range printed on the can. Use the same crayoning and testing routine as with the two-wax system. Remember, backcountry waxing doesn't require a magician. This four- or five-wax approach satisfies the backcountry skier's need for ultralight weight with plenty of versatility.

A note about newer techniques: in firm spring conditions I have gone on long tours with no kick wax at all—just a pair of skating skis, a belt pack, and long skating poles. Skating isn't just for racing. It's very effective in the backcountry, especially for long, gradual grades—those deemed interminable when striding or double-poling. But to skate you do need firm conditions. Frozen corn in the backcountry is ideal; skating in a foot of fresh powder isn't. It's plodding. So add skating equipment and technique to your repertoire, but carry kick wax—and skins—for the wide variety of conditions prevalent in the bush.

Skins

Today, if you talk about waxing for the backcountry, you have to talk about skins. Originally called "sealskins" (that's what they were made from), climbing skins have become an indispensable part of the backcountry skier's kit. More and more backcountry skiers are relying on skins. For long climbs, they are the ticket. Skins provide purchase for straight climbing where waxed (or waxless) skis would require herringbone or side-step.

Can you travel only with skins? For straight-up, straight-down tours I just carry skins; but for longer tours that involve flats, I carry both skins and wax. Skins grip like Velcro® but have little glide. If your tour involves some long flats, even if it's on heavy tele or randonnée gear, a can of grip wax can be a godsend.

The two most popular skins are strap-on plastic skins and the many varieties of plush pile skins. The latter is the most common worldwide, made from a synthetic and/or mohair plush pile that is designed to perform like the natural seal skin. With hairs that point back, the skin can slide forward; but when pushed back, the hairs are pushed against their grain to dig into the snow surface. Mohair skins are said to glide better in cold weather. Synthetic skins are generally more durable. Both types of plush perform very well.

Skins come in different widths for different-width skis. I rely on skins for uncompromising grip, and for this reason I carry skins that cover the ski from edge to edge at its narrowest point. Some skiers use narrower skins on wide skis for more glide, but grip is compromised, not only in straight climbing but in traverses. If your skins don't extend right up next to the edge, you lose the plush's grip when traversing firm snow. For acceptable grip, skins should be no narrower than two-thirds of the ski's width at its narrowest point.

Plush skins have several different forms of attachment. By far my favorite is the stick-on variety, but you have to take care of them. Stick-on skins have a renewable, multiuse adhesive that sticks to a clean ski base with very little additional hardware. Their advantage is that, when properly applied, they do not accumulate snow underneath and slip sideways, and they leave your ski edges free for side-stepping and hard-snow traverses. Their disadvantage is that the adhesive must be kept clean and renewed; and in very cold weather, the adhesive needs to be kept warm— close to the body—for it to work well.

Most adhesive skins have tip loops and tail hooks, with elastic at one end or the other. If properly glued this hardware isn't necessary, but it does help keep the skins from sliding off of the tail. With an elastic/tail-hook system, it's important not to adjust the skin length too short; you'll put too much tension on the skin adhesive. If my skis don't have a tail notch, I carefully file one into the tail protector to give the tail hook a place to nest. I also have a roll of white first-aid tape in my pack in case of an unexpected skin delamination.

If you choose stick-on skins, take care of them. Scrape excess wax off of your skis—especially soft kick waxes. Wipe the ski base clean of dirt and moisture before putting on the skins. When carrying skins, fold them back on themselves, adhesive-against-adhesive, so that your stickum is not contaminated (see illus.27). During application, be careful not to drop your skins in the pine needles.

27
Folding skins

The skins' adhesive will remain effective for many applications. How many depends on temperature and how clean you keep them. I reglue my skins before any big trip, and if it's much more than 7 to 10 days, I carry an extra tube of glue. For shorter trips carry a roll of adhesive tape and maybe a can of spray glue to touch up small slippery spots.

Regluing skins is like applying klister on a squirmy, moving target. The ideal way to apply a new coat of glue is to duct-tape your skins by the tip and tail attachments, glue-side up, to an easily cleaned workbench or tabletop. Be sure to pull them tight. Old glue can be warmed with a hair dryer and carefully removed with a scraper. New glue should be warm when applied. Deposit a bead sparingly in the center of the skin and spread it with a klister spreader. If this sounds like a mess, many shops—and some skin distributors—are set up to reglue your skins for a nominal fee.

Strap-on plush skins' main advantage is that they require less attention and care. If you don't think you'll take care of adhesive skins, choose these. They're pretty idiot-proof; you can even strap them over sticky wax. Their disadvantage is that their attachment straps cover the edge of the ski and compromise edging. They can also accumulate snow between the ski base and skin, and can rotate sideways on the ski. Strap-on skins do not traverse well; and unless they have metal attachments that strap around the edge, the edges eventually wear through the straps.

Plastic skins are made from a stretchy plastic that has grippers molded into the plastic like plush pile's hairs. They are very grippy, with no glide. They work best for those who use skins only for the steepest climbs. Their advantages are ease of adjustment, price, and ease of care—they, too, can be strapped on right over your kick wax. They do not absorb nor are they affected by moisture. Their disadvantages are the lack of glide—they turn your skis into long snowshoes—and like plush strap-ons, the straps go over the edges, and snow can accumulate between ski and skin. These skins, too, aren't made for traversing.

TUNING YOUR SKIS

Most of us are familiar with tuning our skiing technique, but many of us neglect our equipment. Sure, technique problems are usually caused by operator error, not the skis. But neglecting your skis' tuning can compound those errors. It doesn't take much to keep your skis properly tuned. With a few tools and a little time you can get your new skis ready to turn or buff out your old skis as good as new. Once tuned, your skis will be much easier to maintain for optimum performance.

The simplest solution to ski tuning is taking your skis to a qualified ski service shop and having them stone ground. It's not cheap, but if this is the route that you choose, remember that both grinders and operators are not created equal. Ask around; see where the local hotshots and alpine racers go *before* you relinquish your skis to the robo machine. (When I have my skis ground, I prefer a flat base with a 1-degree base-edge bevel; see below.)

Getting a Flat Base

Your ski's base should be flat; if part of the base is high or low you won't get the most out of your investment. Many skis come excessively base-high from the factory, giving the ski bottom a convex shape. Base-high skis are squirrelly and unstable. But skis with high bases are easier to ski than those with low or concave bases; this so-called "railed" phenomenon makes any ski desperately unpredictable.

To determine if your bases are flat, first check them with a *true bar*—a metal bar machined perfectly flat for eyeballing bases and edges (see illus. 28). Hold the ski up to the light and move the true bar down the

28
Checking for a flat base with a true bar

full length of the ski, looking for daylight between the ski base and the bar. Light will show where the base or the metal edges are low. No light will show through spots that are flat or too high. High bases should be scraped or ground down; skis with high edges should be filed flat.

As I mentioned earlier, if your skis' plastic bases are excessively high it's best to have them stone ground by a qualified tuning shop. Of course, such luxuries aren't always available. If that's the case, you can scrape the skis with a metal scraper until they are flat. To flatten a high base, hold your ski securely in ski vises—also support the ski in the middle—and scrape the high spots down with the sharp side of a metal scraper. Tip the scraper away from you and push it using long, even strokes from tip to tail (see illus. 29). (You can sharpen a dull scraper with a file, taking care to keep the scraper edge flat.) Be careful not to flex the scraper. (I like to hold a plastic scraper behind my metal one to help keep it flat.)

29
Flattening a
high base with
a metal
scraper

You should be able to feel it grip those areas of the ski base that are too high. Check the ski base periodically to be sure you aren't removing too much base material. Scrape until the material is perfectly flat and flush with the ski edge.

Flat Filing

Your ski is "railed" when its edges are higher than its base. On a railed ski, light will show between the base and the true bar, but none will show between the edges and the bar. Railed skis can be desperately difficult to turn, and they will "hook" badly when skiing across the fall line. Flat filing solves the problem.

For heavy flat filing use at least a 10-inch-mill bastard file. Some prefer an auto body file or a Panser, but with these aggressive tools you must know when to stop. Whichever file you choose, grip it close to the ski, placing your thumbs over the ski's edges (see illus. 30). Be careful not to

30
Flat filing
your edges

bend the file when you grip it; keep it flat. Place it on the ski at an angle so its teeth cut. You will soon get the feel of the best angle according to the design of your file. You can push or pull the file, whichever seems most comfortable; but the file's tang should always point *away* from the cutting direction.

File with long, smooth strokes. Clean the file often with the brush side of a file card; the metal side dulls files and is best saved for hard-to-remove wax residue and plastic filings. Keep the base of the ski free of filings with a rag or brush. File the edges until they are flush with the base, checking the ski frequently with a true bar.

Beveling the Edge

Alpine skiers are familiar with edge beveling: tuning the ski with its edges filed slightly lower than the level of the plastic base. Beveling is important for telemark skiers, too, since it lowers the grabby edge, making the ski easier to swivel and easing your turn initiation. Beveling reduces that "catchy" feeling so aggravating in three-pin skis and so conducive to outside-edge falls. It minimizes that "too sharp" sensation in soft and crusty snow and on steep slopes; and with beveled edges, experts can ski those skinny boards farther away from their body—like the big boys and girls—rather than using an upright "nordic" stance.

If you're willing to spend the money and you have a trustworthy tuning shop nearby, you can take your skis to be stone ground and edge-beveled precisely to your instructions. My preference is a 1-degree base-edge bevel. This isn't a lot. Some alpine skiers use up to a 3-degree bevel; and many of these "combat" skiers bevel the tips and tails more than the center of the skis. You can experiment with different degrees of bevel, but if you bevel telemark skis too much they'll have to be tipped too far over to engage the edge. Their wide nordic bindings will drag, putting you in a desperate situation on steep, hard snow.

There is no mystery to edge beveling. If you don't have the heavy machinery to do it, you have some simple options. The most foolproof tool for edge beveling at home is a quality hand beveler. If you don't care to buy yet another tool, you can do an effective job with a piece of duct tape on a 10-inch file. If you buy a hand beveler, be sure that it can bevel the base edge; many of them only bevel the side edge. If your beveling tool is adjustable I recommend setting it at 1 degree for beveling the bottom edge of telemark skis. If you choose to bevel your skis more than that you should bevel the side edge, too. This keeps the edge profile close to 90 degrees for the best edge bite. Follow the instructions included with your tool for both procedures.

To bevel with a file and duct tape, carefully wrap the end of your 10-inch or 12-inch file with two wraps of the tape (see illus. 31). Rub the tape flat, making sure there are no raw edges or wrinkles. Place the file on the ski with the tape over one edge, the file over the other edge. The tape will lift one side of the file so that it tunes the opposite edge with a slight bevel. File with long, smooth strokes, just as you did when you were flat filing. You can monitor your edge bevel by the new metal that is exposed as you file; or, if you're not sure of yourself, use a side-filing trick: color the edge with a felt-tipped marker before filing. Be careful to keep the ink off of your clear plastic base because it can stain it. File until the full width of the edge is beveled. It's also best to bevel into the base for about an edge-width. Now turn the file around and repeat the process on the other edge.

31
Taping your
file for beveling
your edges

By taping your file carefully and replacing the tape if it packs too flat, you can do an excellent job using this method. You'll quickly get the feel of your files and how much they are cutting. Take your time and use your true bar. If you remove too much metal you'll have to scrape the base down and start all over.

Side Filing

Telemark skis should have offset edges like alpine skis. When you hit a rock, the metal edge is work-hardened by the impact. The result is a rough spot called a *burr,* and it's usually much harder than the rest of the edge. You may have the same problem with a new ski whose edges have been work-hardened by the manufacturer's final base grinding. With work-hardened edges you can file until you're blue in the face, but you'll make little progress.

You can side-file skis with an offset edge to restore them to 90 degrees and to remove nicks or burrs. First put one of your skis firmly in a vise. You'll need both a stone and a file. Go over these areas with a stone first. You'll reduce the hard spot so that your file will bite. It's worth taking this extra step to minimize wear on yourself and your files.

For shorter, more flexible files, hold the file in the palm of your hand and run it lengthwise along the side edge in long, smooth strokes (see illus. 32). Be sure to keep the file flat against the edge and sidewall. If it's a bigger, more rigid file you can hold it in both hands at an angle to the edge as though you are flat filing. You will need to keep your thumbs pressed right over the edge to keep from bending the file. It is important to file evenly and perpendicular to the ski base. If the new metal is exposed evenly along the full width of the edge, you are doing fine. This is a great place for the felt-tipped marker trick: color the side edge and then file the ink off evenly.

After sharpening your edges you should remove the burr created by the file and then dull the edges back from the tips and tails. The too-sharp burr will hang up the skis in turns, and the skis will behave as though they were railed. I prefer a burr stick for removing the burr. A burr stick is a "rubber stone," like an eraser with just the right amount of abrasiveness to remove the burr without losing the keen edge.

If you have a burr stick, run it along the edges tip-to-tail. If you don't, lightly run a fine whetstone or emery paper the full length of the edge at a 45-degree angle to the ski base. Then use your burr stick or stone to dull the edges back 15 centimeters from the contact surface of each ski's tip and tail. It is a good idea to carry some emery paper or a small pocket stone. Diamond stones are great for this application. Depending on the

32
*Side filing
your edges*

snow, you might want to "de-tune" your skis' edges a bit more if they seem catchy.

Once your skis have been properly tuned you will never want to go back to an untuned ski. To keep them at their best, occasionally touch them up with your stone or a light side filing. Keep them sharp, especially underfoot. And stay out of the rocks.

Mount Sopris

We staggered up the talus field in pitch darkness, armed with one very weak and another completely broken headlamp. I must have suffered a memory lapse when I agreed to do this two days in a row. Yesterday we had done the same thing on Mount Daly, stumbling off into the dark with an alpine start. At least yesterday there was a road and a moon—and a great descent.

Two hours later it was as though the talus had never existed. We had other things to worry about as we whacked our way up a near-ice slope.

We finally reached the summit with toes smashed from kicking steps. There was a change in plan; no way were we going to ski the slope we had just ascended. It was a shady sheet of ice.

The other side, in the sun, looked beautiful. It was a vast, open bowl. We relaxed and enjoyed a thermos of tea. I was the first to descend, so I felt I shouldn't break protocol to stop and rest my aching thighs. My turns got bigger and bigger; fortunately the snow was forgiving. That first bowl was the longest, but there was more: little steep shots, trees, meadows—6,000 feet in all.

Back at the road, it took an hour or so to get the truck out of the mud. I knew we had carried those shovels for something. Two switchbacks down the old road, stopping to look back, we spotted another line.

"Hey Michael, do you have to work tomorrow? Maybe we should give that slope a try."

Another memory lapse.

High mountain powder (Rob Bernthal)

TRAINING

I am not into competition, but I like to stay fit because it makes skiing and summer activities more fun. For me, everyday exercise is a necessity like eating and sleeping. That's the spirit of this chapter. We'll be talking about staying fit for better turns and for enjoyment of backcountry skiing—not competitive skiing. If you're competing, I'd recommend a qualified coach and a scientific training schedule to remain injury free and to maintain your best results.

The best training for skiing is skiing, but we all don't have the luxury of skiing year-round. Besides, you need to participate in exercise other than skiing to develop the muscles that aren't so important to turns but that just might stave off fatigue and injury while skiing.

The first criterion for any kind of training is to choose a form of exercise that you enjoy enough to maintain. If you don't like it, you probably won't do it. Another criterion—one to be approached prudently—is specificity: if you have to make maximum use of a limited amount of training time, muscle-specific exercises will produce the greatest benefit. World-class coaches emphasize this training specificity to the extreme because they want their athletes to make the most of every training minute. For example, during "classic-technique" training, cross-country racers don't just go running—they always run with ski poles. For skating, they skate on a slide board or roller skis. The danger of being too specific is that it can be more like work; I try to choose an exercise first because it's fun, second because it's applicable to skiing.

STRETCHING

Stretching before a workout is a great psych-up and helps to prevent muscle injury. You don't need Jane Fonda, Richard Simmons, or sitar music in the background—just a few stretches that are muscle-specific to your sport. It helps to read up on the subject. Bob Anderson's *Stretching* is a classic, an excellent primer. Always start with an easy warm-up before you stretch. This is crucial, since cold muscles don't stretch—they tear.

Ski touring on the Kahn-Tengri Expedition

96

Start easy to get your pulse up and your blood moving. Warm down in the same way, slowing to relax your muscles. Don't cool off too quickly.

ORGANIZING AN EXERCISE SCHEDULE

The more you exercise, the more important it is to rest. Organize your schedule to include both hard and easy days for maximum benefit from your training. Alternate the hard and easy days, and take one complete rest day each week. Otherwise you will become tired and "overtrained." You will rarely be rested enough to push yourself to get the most from each workout.

How long should you exercise each day? You don't have to maintain a rigid schedule to get plenty of positive benefit from training, but some guidelines are helpful. These days coaches acknowledge that quality is more important than quantity. Using a "normal" week as an example, I exercise about an hour each work day and reserve a long, easy workout for Saturday (2 to 3 hours) and a long, hard workout for Sunday (1½ to 2½ hours). Monday is for resting. Climbing or skiing over the weekend counts toward the long workout. Isn't that what you're training for? Monday's rest is certainly crucial for healing overexerted muscles, but I find it even more important for keeping up my interest. Take a day off and you'll be more excited about getting rolling the next day.

It is important to monitor your body during each workout; otherwise you might push harder than you should for a slow "recovery" workout and compromise a hard one; or you might coast through a hard workout and not gain the maximum benefit from it. By checking your pulse rate you can accurately monitor each day's training. Your pulse is the "tachometer" of a workout. It indicates how hard you are pushing your body.

To determine your pulse rate during a workout, stop and count your heartbeats for 15 seconds and multiply that number by four. If you don't want to stop, you can use a pulsemeter. I use one with a wireless sending unit that straps around the chest and a wristwatch that displays my pulse rate. The figure you get from your calculations or pulsemeter should fall within your "training range." If your pulse is too low, you should speed up. If it's too high, ease off a bit.

To estimate your "training range" first determine your maximum pulse rate by subtracting your age from 225. Your training range should fall between 70 percent and 80 percent of the maximum rate. If you are thirty-two, for example, your maximum pulse rate is 193 beats per minute and should range between 135 and 154 during training. Note that this is a rough guideline that varies according to your fitness and the altitude.

On easy days, stay near the lower end of your training range, around 70 percent of your maximum. Concentrate on keeping your pulse down because you want your body to rest for the harder workouts. On hard days get closer to the 80 percent mark, which will mean that your body is approaching its anaerobic threshold: the stage at which you get "pumped." These hard days require the most recovery time.

Once you have a good aerobic base, you can increase your speed through specific training: alternately crossing and retreating from your "anaerobic threshold." With this kind of training your body will grow accustomed to a higher energy output and greater speed. A spontaneous sort of speed training that I enjoy is called *fartlek,* a Swedish term for speed play. During *fartlek* you increase your speed at random and slow the pace for recovery when you tire. For instance, when on my bicycle on a course with rolling hills I jam on the ups and rest on the downs. Cross-country ski courses tend to force these kinds of demands on the skier: shorter, intense pushes up hills with fast glides down.

A more regimented kind of speed training is "intervals." When doing intervals you closely monitor alternating periods of high-energy output and recovery. With anaerobic intervals you extend yourself past your 80 percent mark for a short time (usually between 30 seconds and 3 minutes), then slow for recovery until your pulse drops to 100 beats. Time the recovery period: when it takes markedly longer than the first interval for your pulse to drop, you have done enough intervals.

For intervals—and any kind of speed training—it is important to be well rested and have a good training base. Warm up, stretch, and warm down. Start off with very short intervals, and don't push too hard. Too little speed training won't do you any harm—it is too much speed training that injures many athletes. Consult a good running, cycling, or ski racing book to set up a speed-training schedule.

CROSS-COUNTRY AND IN-LINE SKATING

The evolution of classic cross-country technique to skating has done more to improve my downhill skiing than any other activity. The movements for snow skating are easy to duplicate on pavement. It's not only fun but it's muscle-specific for downhill as well as cross-country ski training. Skates with in-line wheels or roller skis designed for skating are your best choice for skate training. Add long cross-country skating poles and you will effectively train your upper as well as your lower body. There are several good books on skating available. Find one you like. Find a smooth pavement, too—you will feel every bump on those tiny wheels.

STRENGTH TRAINING

I keep trying to convince my girlfriend that aerobic athletes must be scrawny to be good—especially when she's gawking at my buddies' biceps and thighs. It's true that skiers need strength for leg-pumping crud, packing a big load into a backcountry cabin, or squeezing off that last desperate turn. Most important, specific-strength training makes a skier more resistant to injury. Pushups, situps (the abdomen is especially important to skiers), pullups, and all sorts of calisthenics are simple, effective strength builders. Today's gyms usually have a resident body builder who can set you up with a good program, and most importantly, with the right technique.

It usually takes some kind of toy or apparatus to keep me interested in strength training my legs. Nautilus is a great workout, but it isn't always available and is not very portable. For maximum portability there are several stretch devices for strength and flexibility training. These are tools that, when attached to a fixed object, can be pulled in different directions to exercise specific muscles.

My favorite of these is the Sport Cord. It was introduced to me by U.S. Ski Team Trainer John Atkins as part of my recuperative program after knee surgery. A very simple, portable training device, the Sport Cord was developed for athletes' specific-strength training and is used both as a preventative against injury and as part of a recuperative program after injury. It provides a great workout.

Regardless of your choice of exercise, keeping yourself excited about being fit is the key to success. Choose training activities that are fun, like skating and cycling, and that exercise the right muscle groups for skiing. Rest to preserve your enthusiasm for each session, and alternate the difficulty of various sessions. You will find yourself more fit and your skiing more fun and enjoyable.

Descent from Mount Aspiring on French Ridge in New Zealand

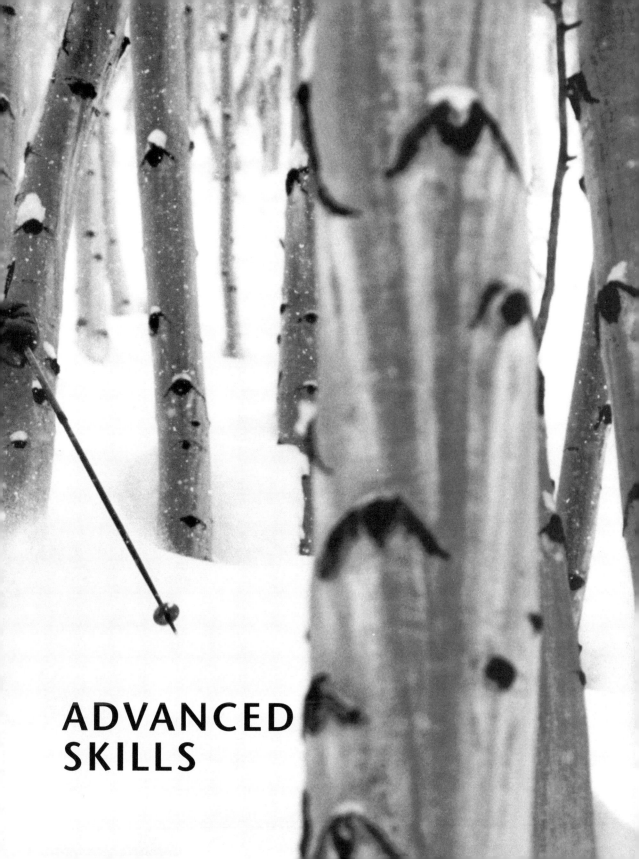

ADVANCED
SKILLS

SKATING

Last season I geared up with wrist guards and two sets of knee pads and started snowboarding. Dude! Grays on trays *rule!*

The one thing that I miss while snowboarding, however, besides the necessary boundless enthusiasm to hammer myself, is being able to *skate.* Having your feet committed to one plank makes it impossible. Not only is skating an important edging exercise for skiers; it's the best means of propulsion on slippery, downhill-waxed skis.

Learn to skate on your tele skis. I use the skate everywhere: traversing cat roads, accelerating on flat downhills, transportation from one lift to another. In the backcountry, an efficient skate on your tele or randonnée boards can quickly get you past what would be interminable flats, plodding with skins on your skis.

If you want to get into skating for its own sake, try cross-country ski skating. There are good books available on the different techniques. For now I'll outline simple skating on heavy, metal-edged boards.

33
Skating on
tele skis

SKATING EXERCISES

Start by practicing the herringbone (see the chapter Basic Parallel Turns). Once that feels comfortable, change terrain to a *very gradual* uphill. This will allow you to get a bit of *glide.* Now, as you step from one ski to the other, give a little push to glide on the new ski. You should be using the same duck-footed position as with the herringbone, but push a little harder from one ski to the other, and let each ski glide before the next push.

Now try the next step: as you push off of one ski onto the other (gliding) ski, try to put the gliding ski down on its *outside* edge. That's right, its outside edge. Transfer your weight *completely* to that gliding ski—no hanging back on the pushing one.

OK, now the flats. Pick a flat, hard-packed area. On the hill, it was

Pages 102–103:
Colorado
powder

probably hard to actually put your gliding ski down on its outside edge, but thinking about the outside edge got your ski *flat* so that it would glide. In the flats, you can really do it. See how in illustration 33 the skier comes down on that ski on its outside *edge*. The weight shifts from the pushing ski to the outside edge of the gliding ski. Then that gliding ski is rolled over onto its inside edge for the next push.

If you feel like you're "stuck" between your feet, try making more of a V with your skis and push from one side of the V to the other. Let your body sway side to side, from your pushing edge to your gliding edge, and *completely commit your weight* to that outside gliding edge. Drive your hips directly over the new gliding ski with each skate.

As you get your weight shift down, you can push off on your poles at the same time. Downhill-length poles aren't the best for skating—they're too short for much power—but they will add a bit of balance and rhythm to your skate. Pushing on your poles with each skating motion on each side is what cross-country skiers call *V2*.

Here's another exercise. Focusing on the inside and outside corners of your boots, try skating from the *inside corner* of the boot on your pushing ski to the *outside corner* of the boot on your gliding ski. For some skiers, especially those with stiff boots, it's easier to use this *inside corner, outside corner* approach (see "The Inside Corner" in the chapter Advanced Parallel Tips).

KEY SKATING POINTS

Skating is a natural movement that most of us have practiced during our first or subsequent childhoods on roller skates, in-line skates, ice skates, alpine skis, or skating skis. Skating on these tele boards is no different. The key points are as follows:

- Make a shallow V with your skis—be sure that they aren't parallel.
- Make a *complete* weight shift from pushing to gliding ski.
- Put the gliding ski down on (or almost on) its *outside edge*.
- Feel the pressure on the *inside corner* of your pushing boot, the *outside corner* of your gliding boot.

Perfect your skating and you'll learn to control your edges. As your gliding ski becomes your new pushing ski, you'll feel yourself roll from its outside gliding edge to its inside pushing one. You'll feel the total commitment from pushing edge to gliding edge. This is key in advanced skiing and a major emphasis in this book: learning to control not only the outside ski in a turn, but the inside ski and its uphill edge. Controlling that uphill, or inside, ski and its edge opens the door to expert teles and parallel turns.

ADVANCED TELEMARK TIPS

In the early telemark days, the back ski acted as a rudder while the front ski did most of the work. A flatter, less-weighted back ski created elegant, long-radius arcs in soft snow but was a disaster on harder snow. That is probably one reason why the telemark had a short first life. As soon as Rudolph Lettner, an Austrian metal worker, put metal edges on a pair of skis and skiers like Hannes Schneider got hold of a pair, telemark was put out to pasture and skiers were rippin', arcing the Arlberg.

In these modern days of telemark, skiers are determined to ski all conditions using the genuflecting turn, so technique has had to evolve. So has equipment: plastic boots and sophisticated alpine-like skis flexed for the telemark turn facilitate arcs that rival any alpine turn—*if* you don't neglect that back ski.

TUCKING YOUR BACK LEG

When I think of a series of good tele turns, I think of a horse. I liked horses before I discovered skis. When I really wanted to get my horse—his name was John—to perform, I would first get him collected. I would rein him in, signaling him to prepare for anything: a quick turn, a jump, a skid-stop. John knew the signal. He would collect his big body into a "ready" posture rather than trotting along, spread out. He would perk up as though he had just seen a snake and was preparing to bolt.

In your telemark, try "collecting" yourself by tucking your rear leg under you and bringing your body into its most athletic position. Don't leave your back leg flapping in the breeze like a wounded dog (a doggie leg); keep it under you where you can use it (see illus. 34). Like John's, your body should feel collected and ready to bolt. It's that athletic position that we discussed earlier in the book: stomach in, lower back relaxed.

Try pinching your buttocks together as though you are holding a C-note between your cheeks. This helps tuck that leg and tighten your stance fore-to-aft. You'll feel aggressive, ready for anything.

Anticipation

34
**Tuck your
rear leg**

POINTING YOUR KNEE

Telemark or parallel, I do a lot of pointing with my knees. You'll pick up these "pointy-knee" ideas throughout this book. Some coaches call them "sharp knees."

Start your turns thinking of your front knee as a headlight. With each turn sweep the headlight beam toward your new destination. This focus will enhance the edging and steering of your front ski.

Now try thinking of your *back knee* as the headlight. Forget your front one for a minute; point your back (inside) knee into the new turn. Once the front knee/headlight becomes automatic, I prefer to focus on this back knee (see illus. 35).

35
Point your
front and your
back knees
into the turn

USING YOUR BIG TOE, LITTLE TOE

This is something that sticks in many of my students' minds: "big toe, little toe." The big-toe, little-toe idea is simple: when you edge your skis into a turn, you should feel the pressure under the big-toe side (inside-edge side) of your front foot and the little-toe side (outside-edge side) of your rear foot. This will edge your skis properly. Note that it's not just the big toe and little toe that get the focus: it's that whole *side* of each foot that edges the ski.

For most skiers it's the little-toe part of this idea that really gets results. Thinking about the weight under the *little-toe side* of that back foot edges your back (uphill) ski (see illus. 36). Edging and weighting your back ski is the key to preventing those "spinning out" turns.

36
Edge on the big-toe side of your front foot and the little-toe side of your back foot

Mick Wheeler, Envers du Plan, Chamonix

Be aware of your foot position on your rear ski; avoid "tiptoeing" on it, hinging your boots up on their toes. Keep your entire forefoot on the ski.

If you feel the rear ski sliding out from under you, concentrate more pressure on the little-toe side of the rear foot. If you have trouble initiating your turns (a less frequent problem), concentrate more pressure on the big-toe side of the front foot.

DROPPING YOUR REAR HEEL

In the Basic Telemark chapter you learned to emphasize the *weight* on your inside (rear) ski. Now I've added "big-toe, little-toe," the little-toe idea further emphasizing *edging* the rear ski. *Weighting and edging* the rear ski in your telemark will give you better control of your turn.

Your rear ski should bear at least half of your body weight—it seems like even more in certain kinds of snow. You can tell that you have enough weight back there when you feel the Achilles tendon and calves of your rear leg stretch. You will automatically tuck your hips under you to ease that tension.

For your next telemark turn go one step further. *Relax and bend your rear ankle* so your heel drops closer to the ski. Stay on edge, of course; but try to get as much of your rear foot onto the ski as possible (refer back to illus. 35). The more foot you have on that back ski the more weight it gets, and the better you will be able to control it through the finish of each turn.

DOING MORE WITH YOUR HIPS

An expert tele skier will look very similar to an alpine skier—from the waist up. The quiet upper body is always facing down the hill. But the radical differences between the leads of the two turns result in two very different postures from the waist down.

In alpine skiing the pelvis faces more directly down the hill—the hips are "open" to the hill—with the uphill ski ahead of the downhill one. A tele skier, however, has the downhill ski advanced, so the hips rotate with the turn rather than facing downhill. I think of it as "punching" my downhill hip around.

In illustration 37 notice how the tele skier's hips punch through the turn, setting the skis on their edges and using the big hip muscles to keep them there. His upper body acts as though it's separated from his lower body, facing quietly downhill as the skis arc back and forth. As I punch this hip around, I feel the pressure under the *arch* of my front foot.

When you use your hips to turn you must *concentrate even more on*

*37
Tele-
anticipation:
chest facing
down the hill,
hips cranking
the turn*

facing your torso down the hill. When you make a turn, the downhill hip rotates and your torso twists the other way. With skis and hips turning, chest and navel always facing the fall line, your body acts as a coiled spring ready to be released. When you release your edges, those stretched back muscles and contracted stomach muscles whip your skis into the next arc. Your turns snap around effortlessly from all of that stored energy.

This is *tele-anticipation*—upper body and hands always facing down the hill in anticipation of the new turn. In this position I feel my abdomen getting a workout: the downhill (outside) muscles of my abdomen contracted, the uphill muscles of my abdomen (and lower back) stretched.

Use your abdomen as much as you can. The more you anticipate, especially with the tele's advanced outside hip, the more your abdomen will work for you. If you feel your abdominal muscles in each turn, then you are probably doing it right.

TIMING YOUR EDGING

If you initiate your teles by stemming a front ski and *then* transferring weight to the rear ski, you're doing a two-step kind of turn. Technicians call this a "sequential turn initiation" because the skis are edged in a one-two sequence. This "step-telemark" is covered later in this book. It is one of those sequential turns used for moguls and hairy terrain. Its quick directional change allows you to "walk" down otherwise formidable slopes. I do not recommend it as your standard turn.

I prefer to edge my skis *at the same time* in a "simultaneous turn initiation." It's a bit more difficult but much more fluid and effective in working the skis. It carves them, as opposed to turning them with one-two moves that use stepping, steering, and skidding.

Try this more fluid series of movements the next time you link teles. As you rise between turns, keep both skis flat—in "neutral"—during your lead change. Once the correct foot is forward for the new turn, put it in gear and *edge both skis at the same time* for the next turn. Tip the skis over, pressuring them under the *big-toe side* of your front foot and the *little-toe side* of your rear foot—*at exactly the same time*.

Simultaneous edging is a very smooth style of skiing (see illus. 38). With it, you can often eliminate stepping to feel your way into questionable snow conditions. You'll more confidently arc through difficult snow.

The next step in timing your edging focuses on the start of the turn. When initiating the turn, try to initiate it with the *uphill edge of your back ski*—your "little-toe" ski. Do this by trying to make that back-ski edge *the first thing that contacts the snow* when you change leads.

Earlier in this chapter, I said *edge at the same time;* now I'm trying to get on that edge even sooner. It helps some advanced skiers to think of this as *dropping their rear leg back* into a tele as they start the turn rather than moving the front leg forward. This way, that rear leg already has the focus.

Don't worry about the front ski for now; for most advanced telemark skiers the front ski's edging and steering is an automatic movement in their lead change. Focus on edging and weighting that back ski. You don't need to lean back—keep your body position normal. Just drop that foot back into a tele, and get on that edge earlier.

Why? With this exercise you can avoid sequential movements to initiate the turn: that "one-two" stepping movement that some skiers use when they edge the front ski first, then edge and finish the arc on the back ski. That takes more time. I'd rather get both skis arced and turning together. Focusing on edging your back ski *first* really gets both skis edging and turning *at the same time*. I've found that when I use this focus on

38
Edge both skis
at the same
time

hard snow or in grabby, tricky snow, my skis will pick the same arc rather than converging or diverging as they so often do in crud—especially using one-two moves.

Try it. Go out and make some arcs focusing on turn initiation with that *back-ski edge*.

Now try *steering* that back ski. Steer it—twist it—with your forefoot into the new turn as you edge it. It's a different feel from steering a ski with your heel down, as in a wedge turn; you direct the ski with your forefoot. *Edge it* and *steer it* with your forefoot at the initiation of your turn.

As you add this back-ski emphasis, especially once you steer your back ski, you'll find your skis drifting apart a little, widening your stance. You might even feel that the front and back skis are *diverging* a bit, rather than the common converging (wedging) that characterizes most skiers' telemarks. That's good. A wider stance will help you edge and steer your skis equally into each new turn. Through the turn, keep weighting, steering, and edging that back ski, and your skis will stay wider, more parallel. This wider, parallel-ski tele stance is more effective not only in soft and difficult snow, but on hard snow, allowing you to better edge the back skis with a more stable side-to-side platform.

It's unlikely, but if you find yourself doing a "wheelie" with an ineffectual front ski, make a few of your normal turns to get back into a rhythm, then focus on the back-ski edge. Feel how much more you can use the back ski, rather than trailing it behind into the finish of the turn. In advanced skiing, your back ski—or inside ski in parallel—is an important tool to build the right angles between the snow, your edges, and the rest of your body.

BACK SKI REVIEW

In alpine turns you vary your weight distribution between skis according to the snow conditions. Often—especially on hard snow—you're skiing with your weight on one ski at a time. Telemark, however, is almost always a two-ski turn. I've given the back ski a lot of emphasis in this assortment of ski tips not because it's more important than the front ski, but because it's the most often neglected.

Below is a summary of the pointers that I've given above. These exercises will help you weight, control, and arc your back ski. There are a lot of different tips listed. In an on-snow class, it would take at least a couple of days to present all of them—and much longer for the students to practice and absorb them. Be patient; take your time. It's important to think about these things *one at a time*. They all are exercises to achieve the same end—controlling and using the rear ski—so choose the one that works best for you. Refer to the illustrations in this chapter for a good image.

- Tuck your leg. If you feel as if your telemark stance is too long and spread out, you may not be able to properly weight the back ski. Notice how in illustration 34 the skier's rear leg is tucked under the body so that it can be weighted, not so far back that he's up on his tiptoes. Think of pointing that back knee straight down at the ski; or, pinch your buttocks together and your legs will naturally come together into a more "collected" stance.
- Point your front knee like a headlight, shining it into each new turn.
- Point your back knee like a headlight, shining it into each new turn (illus. 35).

- Think "big toe, little toe." Feel pressure on your edges under the big-toe side of your front foot, the little-toe side of your back foot (illus. 36).
- Drop your heel. Think of dropping your back heel closer to the ski, pressing on the ball of your back foot (little-toe side) instead of cranking up on your toes. Keep as much of that back foot on the ski as you can (illus. 35).
- Relax and bend the ankle of your back leg through the turn. Flex it as much as you can. This will drop your heel and allow you to get more pressure on the ball of that rear foot.
- Try edging both skis at the same time, emphasizing the *uphill edge of the back ski* (illus. 38).
- When initiating a turn, *slide your rear foot back* rather than your front foot forward. This will keep you centered between your skis rather than too far forward and will keep your rear ski doing much more of the work. It also helps on very steep slopes, reducing that feeling of "diving" down the hill and accelerating uncontrollably.
- Once you are very comfortable with edging both skis at the same time, try *initiating your turns with the inside edge of your back ski.* Your front ski's steering and edging should be a reflex action by now; think about your rear ski and starting your turns with the inside edge of that ski. Are you using both skis? Get the most from them; get your money's worth. There's no sense in just using half a pair. Pressure, weight, and arc that back ski for rounder, more controlled turns. You won't believe the difference.

Ankles on the Jamtal

The wind whistled all night. Morning dawned one of those weird, hazy days in the Alps that signals a big change. On days like that it either clears or it hits the fan, but it doesn't stay the same. We got an early start, crunching over the bulletproof crust. Our group moved fast; we had a long day ahead and didn't want to get stuck in the fog on a featureless glacier. It had snowed just enough to drift into dense, impenetrable booby traps that could disappear in flat light.

We climbed the pass between the Swiss Tuoi hut toward the Austrian Jamtal hut. Climbing was a little scary, the wind's loading having left perfect man-traps that could break loose and carry a skier rapidly over the steep, hard crust underneath. Starting a little avalanche wouldn't be such a big deal, but on the exposed climb an unarrested slide could be serious.

On top of the Jamjoch began the Jamtal Ferner (glacier), stretching down to the Jamtal hut. It was a long, medium-angle slope, not many crevasses, perfect on a powder day, questionable after last night's wind. Our descent was on the lee side of the pass, on the Swiss-Austrian border.

As we peeled off our skins, we surveyed our descent. The glacier was covered with powder artfully sculpted into sastrugi ridges. It looked difficult, so we mulled over technique tricks for staying upright. It was a custom among our group—old ski buddies—to discuss which was the key turn or move from our bag of survival-skiing tricks. Sort of like which wine would be the best with dinner.

Ankles. That was the key.

We've always been told to bend our knees. Knees allow the legs to function as pistons and shock absorbers, extending to pressure and arc the ski, flexing to lighten and absorb that pressure. Yet for me, it's thinking about my ankles that bends my knees. Parallel or telemark, with relaxed ankles that are extended and flexed through the turn, my knees bend naturally and my body stays centered over the skis.

Evaluating the smooth, windblown, trackless snow below, we agreed that ankles it was. Before talking further, I checked out the snow, making a few "demo" turns, exaggerating the flexing and extending of my ankles. It worked; my skis scribed round, controlled turns through the stiff, windblown powder.

Mountains in Europe are big, with lots of vertical. Below us was the Jamtal Ferner's 3,000-foot glacier descent—plenty of room for practice. After too much discussion, each of us got our cranky old ankles moving. The snow was interesting—skiable. Ankles got us arcing turns until, breathless, we had to stop. We kept telling ourselves as our legs got pumped that we needed to use the full range of motion in our ankles to extend and absorb through the turns. For the last fifty turns we could smell the hot soup; we were ready for a break before the long slog up the last pass. There was plenty of time to think about the breakable-crust move we'd need as the sun dropped behind the ridge for our last descent.

Mark Twight, Argentière Glacier

ADVANCED PARALLEL TIPS

Parallel turns are much more effective than telemarks on hard snow or in narrow and precipitous terrain. When you must face the fall line on a steep slope, the parallel turn's stance is stronger and more stable than the rotated position of the telemark. So even if it's not telemarker's dogma, *to be as versatile as possible* you can and should perfect your parallel turns.

Work on your basic parallel and accumulate some mileage. Make enough parallel turns so that you can use them on any moderate terrain. Practice your stem christies, which are useful when you need a very quick turn initiation. Once you've logged those miles, the next step is to develop your all-terrain parallel. You will want to make parallel turns in difficult conditions. You will want to make them instinctively.

To hone your turns we'll work on these things: flexing your ankles, timing your edge change, directing your uphill knee, and feeling your edge under a certain part of your foot. As we did in the tele section, we'll switch the focus from the outside ski to the inside ski. These are all tricks that will transform your basic parallel turns into dependable, all-terrain maneuvers.

USING YOUR ANKLES

Alpine instructors always tell students to bend their knees. Knees, when flexed, act as shock absorbers. Bending them lowers your center of balance and increases your stability. Without knee bend you couldn't flex and extend your legs to weight and unweight your skis and control your edge pressure. Articulating your knees also facilitates angulation, both at the knee joints and at the hips.

Bend your knees, everyone.

But that's not the whole point of my focus. You must also bend your *ankles*. If you bend your knees and not your ankles you'll fall on your butt. More realistically, without flexible ankles your "shock absorbers" disappear. Your skis skid. With every little variation in the snow your weight goes **Which foot** to the extremes, either too far forward or too far back. You try to compen-**forward?** sate, and your body bends at the waist—that's the "feeding-chicken" stance.

120

Ankle bend is an especially important focus for anyone with plastic boot cuffs—alpine or tele—because the cuffs' stiffness takes a more concerted effort to flex. It's easy to spot skiers whose boots are too stiff. They are broken at the waist, clucking down the hill.

Let's ski and think about ankles. Relax in your athletic, rounded ski stance: stomach in, back relaxed. Push off down the slope and gain some momentum. Start with medium-radius, "skiddy" parallel turns, concentrating on smoothly extending and flexing your *ankles* as you extend and sink through each arc. Extend your legs at the beginning of the turn by extending both of your ankles. Doing this I feel centered, pushing down on my toes as I make this extension. At the high point of your "standing up," your extension, begin to sink through the rest of the turn, again *at the ankles* (see illus. 39). Finish with ankles totally flexed. Again you'll be centered; avoid finishing the turns on your toes or heels.

Keep making these skiddy parallels, exaggerating the ankle movement. In stiffer boots it helps to think about *pulling up on your toes* to get a good bend in your ankles as you sink through the turn.

You're on a packed slope, so your weight emphasis should be on your outside foot. Try to feel your weight on your *whole* outside foot—not just on your toes or heel.

MAKING SMOOTHER TURNS

Basic parallel turns are very abrupt and use lots of hard steering movements. Everything happens at once. But in all but the smoothest groomed snow conditions, free-heel skiers can't afford these edge-catching, exaggerated movements. Free-heel parallels have to be smooth, extra efficient.

You can pull off a smooth and elegant parallel turn by shifting your weight to the uphill ski earlier, *before* starting the next turn. Try it. Begin with a traverse, pushing off to gain a little speed. Now stand up tall and shift your weight to the *uphill edge of your uphill ski.* Once you have shifted weight to that uphill edge, *then*—no earlier!—tip the ski over into a turn, rolling it onto its inside edge for your next turn. Voila! It becomes your outside ski. Feel how your body seeks the fall line as you smoothly change edges and steer both skis into the turn. Don't resist; let your body succumb to gravity, down the fall line.

Try it again. Sink through your last turn. As your skis come across the hill and your body finishes its sinking motion, immediately start the rise back up. Stand up tall; when your lower leg is extended, continue your upward movement by shifting to the *uphill edge of your uphill ski.* Once you're shifted to that uphill ski's edge, *then* move into the next turn:

39
**Extend and flex
your ankles**

focus your eyes down the hill and let your body move ahead of your skis, in the new direction (see illus. 40).

If you can think of moving your *body* into the new turn, your skis will tip over automatically. If it's too abstract for you to think of what your body is doing, think of *tipping* the uphill ski over into the new turn, or *rolling it* onto its inside edge. Either way you want to think about it, the move into the new turn starts *after* you've shifted your weight to the *uphill edge of the uphill ski.* Practice on a roomy slope; be patient; and don't start that new turn until your weight is shifted.

FOCUSING ON THE INSIDE SKI

In the telemark section I really emphasized the back foot, the *inside* foot. That is an obvious focus for tele skiers; when you don't use that foot, you spin out.

The inside ski is no less necessary for parallel skiing. We neglect that ski in parallel instruction because the first big hurdle is getting skiers to shift

*40
Shift your
weight to your
uphill ski be-
fore starting
the next turn*

their weight confidently to the outside ski. Once you get over that hurdle and develop a weight shift, it doesn't mean that you can ski only on your weighted outside ski and forget the inside one. On the contrary, the inside ski is an important key to the most advanced turns. Although many of the exercises and drills that instructors use focus on the *outside* foot, you **must** use your inside ski. An inside ski focus—knowing what to do with it—will transform your turns from tentative tacks to confident arcs.

In the following section of tips, I want you to forget your outside ski for awhile. As we did in the advanced telemark turns, let's assume (can we?) that you've practiced enough so that your outside ski is getting the weight and edging that it needs, with movements almost automatic. We'll shift our emphasis to the inside ski to develop your bombproof parallel.

Focus on Your Inside Knee

Have you crossed your tips making parallel turns? It's hard to get a good edge set on the topsheet of your bottom ski. It happens to the best skiers; often they accidentally cross their tips because they're overemphasizing the outside foot and forgetting the inside one, enthusiastically skiing the outside ski right over the top of it. In a steep couloir, that's a bummer.

Your inside ski must be *steered* (twisted to point it in the desired direction) and *edged* (tipped onto its edge) just like the outside ski. By focusing on your inside *knee,* you set up your body for quicker, easier moves.

Think of leading each new turn with your inside knee. Each time you initiate a new turn, focus on pointing the new inside *knee* in the direction of that turn (some call that the *uphill* knee or ski). It might feel as though you are taking a hard corner on a bicycle, leaning into the turn with your inside knee. Emphasizing the inside knee, you'll also point the inside ski's tip in the direction of the new turn (see illus. 41).

This simple steering move with your inside knee, foot, and ski will make your turns much quicker and easier and will eliminate a stemming motion that can result in crossed tips in difficult snow and slides for life on steep terrain. On the steeps, think of "leading," or starting, the turn with that knee. That gets your body aligned for the turn and moves your inside ski out of the way early, so that the outside ski can do its stuff without crossing over it.

Edge Your Inside Ski

Skis that are edged equally are more likely to stay parallel. When you step onto one ski at a time in loose snow your skis tend to wander off in different directions—especially with free heels. On hard snow, unequally edged skis often cross. To avoid the splits or cross-tipped slammers, you must tip both skis over onto their edges *at the same time* (see illus. 41).

Try it: make a series of turns and consciously focus on edging your inside ski. The inside ski doesn't need much weight for this edge to make a difference. Get used to the idea of edging the skis at the *same time*. Don't edge one and then the other. Tip your skis onto their new inside edges *simultaneously*. Note: in deep snow, *edging* doesn't mean that the edge is gripping into firm snow; it means that the ski is tipped over onto its edge. It's still the same movement.

Think "Light as a Feather"

Skiers often ask how much weight they should put on their inside ski during parallel turns. On groomed and firm snow that ski is much lighter than the outside one. This doesn't mean that it's less important; so it's best to work with the last two exercises first before thinking much about weight. Those ideas get us steering and edging the inside ski.

OK, for this exercise on packed, refrozen, or windblown snow, make

41
Point your inside knee (toe and ski tip) into the new turn

parallel turns, thinking "light as a feather" on your inside ski. As you shift your weight to your new outside ski, think *light* on the new inside one. This focus is especially useful in hard conditions when you need a good edge. *Light as a feather.*

Slide the Inside Ski Forward

Sliding this inside foot forward as you finish your turn allows you to get a better edge with both skis. It faces your torso and pelvis into the fall line. Try it. As your skis come out of the fall line, let that inside ski slide forward before you shift your weight to it and start a new turn (again, see illus. 41). Think back to the earlier exercise "making smoother turns." Let that inside ski slide forward as you round your last turn, so that it's *ahead* when you make that early weight shift.

Weight the Inside Ski

We've been working on "light as a feather" on the inside foot. But in different conditions, you will learn to vary this weight distribution. Using a deep-snow parallel, you must put weight on the inside ski so that it doesn't wander with a mind of its own. It's easiest for me to think about my feet: as my skis come into the fall line in deep snow, I *flex my ankles* and pressure that inside foot *on its whole little-toe side*. Try it. Put enough weight on that inside foot to feel pressure on its little-toe side.

Use your inside foot and play with your weight distribution. In light, loose snow you will ski with almost equal weight distribution between your feet. In heavier loose snow, you may put a little more weight on the outside ski. On hard snow, you may have almost *all* your weight on the outside ski. This difference will depend on the heaviness of the snow, the base underneath, and the stiffness of your skis. The goal is the same: to get both skis to arc and float equally. This is done through steering, edging, and weighting (or lightening) the inside ski.

KNEE-TO-BOOT CHASERS

"Knee-to-boot chasers" is an exercise I learned from a member of the PSIA Alpine Demonstration Team. It helps you get your skis out to the side, away from your body, and up on their edges for more carving and less skidding. Knee-to-boot chasers will help you make a more technical turn. Skiing with your feet in a hip-width stance, "chase" your inside (uphill) boot with your outside (downhill) knee. *Tip that inside boot away* so that the knee can't catch it. Notice how your skis are tipped up on their edges (see illus. 42).

THE INSIDE CORNER

Next try a similar idea with a different focus: move into the "inside corner" of your boot. As shown in illustration 43, put your hands on the fronts of your boot cuffs. Now think of your boots as though they have four corners. Move your hands to the inside (or uphill) corner of each boot, as shown in illustration 44. Press your shins toward your hands and toward the uphill corners. This inside corner is where you should press your shins as you move into each new turn.

Now make a series of turns, consciously initiating each by pressing into both *inside corners*—don't press straight forward. Stick with the corners all the way through the turn. Your body should move gracefully into the fall line, the skis well edged throughout the arc.

DRIVING YOUR HEELS

Try a completely different focus: your heels. This is an idea that will get more rebound and snap from advanced turns. Since your heels aren't

43

*Hands on the fronts of
your boot cuffs*

44

*Hands on the "inside corners"; press your shins
toward these corners as you move into a turn*

fastened down, it also helps keep your balance centered in a stable position to reduce the chance of a forward fall.

Carve a few smooth arcs, feeling the weight on your whole outside foot throughout the turn. Now change your focus and think about the heel of your foot. As you round the bend and your skis come out of the fall line, *drive your heels* toward the finish of the arc. That's right. Try to push your heels ahead. Don't sit back. Just think heels, weighting your feet from the arch backward.

These movements don't merely emphasize your feet and legs. By focusing on specific lower-body movements and sensations, your upper body wants to move in the right direction—in the direction of the next turn. You'll soon find yourself seeking the fall line with your torso and skiing more aggressively in the manner described in the chapter Skiing from the Waist Up. Your turns will become indistinguishable from those of a strong alpine skier.

REFINEMENT

MORE FREE-HEEL TURNS

Motion is what makes your skis go round. Flexion and extension lighten and pressure your skis at the proper moment in each arc to get the most from your skis for as little effort as possible.

The low, bent-kneed position of the classic telemark has influenced many free-heel skiers to stay locked in a genuflecting position throughout their tele turns—or stuck in a crouch in parallel turns. *Locked* is the word; there is little maneuverability once down there, and crouching low often results in a pair of sore knees. Bruised and broken patellae are common among low-flying telemarkers whose rear knees skim the snow. Trolling with your kneecaps is a good way to find stumps and rocks.

If you learn to contract and extend your legs, what was once a static, too-low position gives way to a fluid flexion and extension movement. In parallel or telemark turning you need this flexion and extension to control the pressure that builds as your skis come across the fall line. Your skis are most likely to skid at the finish of each turn as they come across the hill. Once across the fall line they resist the force of gravity that is pulling your body downhill and increasing the pressure against your edges. If you do not lighten your skis to absorb this excess pressure they will begin to "chatter."

On hard snow we instinctively want to stiffen and straighten our legs to resist chatter, but the best thing to do is to lighten the skis by flexing at the ankles, sinking and absorbing that pressure on the edges. In order to have the necessary range of motion to make this flexing movement, you should be tall early in the turn—otherwise you will have nowhere to sink.

THE "NOW" TURN

There is a great skiing exercise called the "now" turn (some call it the "patience" turn) to emphasize this feeling of motion. I first learned this exercise from a member of the PSIA Alpine Demonstration Team. I have since used it successfully with many free-heel students with unanimous results. These students improved their turning rhythm, their maneuverability,

Pages 130-131:
Riding the
wave

and their pressure control on their edges. The now turn emphasizes a tall, extended position by delaying the sinking motion until the skis are directly in the fall line.

Find a wide, moderate slope. Using either parallel or telemark turning technique, stand very tall. Stay in this tall position until you reach "now." "Now" is when your skis are in the fall line. Don't sink until your skis are pointing directly down the hill. Say "now" out loud, and sink into the turn finish once your skis are in the fall line. When sinking be sure that you flex at the *ankles and knees,* not at the waist.

Link a sequence of now turns down the hill, concentrating on first standing tall, then delaying the sinking motion. The turns won't be round; they will have a sort of J shape (see illus. 45). You will notice

45
"Now" turns

that the extension-flexion of your legs creates more rhythm in your skiing. Feel how smoothly and crisply your skis finish each turn as the sinking lightens the pressure on your edges and tightens your turn finish. At first the up-and-down motion might feel exaggerated, but you'll soon find that it makes your skis snap around more smoothly and quickly.

Whether you parallel or telemark, the elements are the same. Don't throw out your low position. Ski "through" it with a dynamic, rhythmic flexion and extension motion.

THE TELEMARK TWO-STEP

I'm not wild about "steppy," sequential turns unless you *really* need them. However, the step-telemark is an important technique to have in your quiver, especially for controlled, steered turns on radically steep and bumpy terrain. In grabby crud you can step the front ski across the hill to "feel" the snow, then check your speed with the rear one.

In certain situations it isn't necessarily a regression to choose sequential step-turning techniques rather than simultaneous ones. Sometimes you have to skid your skis in order to turn more quickly. These are spots where, if you spend too much time carving through the fall line, you will pick up uncontrollable speed.

Step-telemarks are a quicker, more advanced version of the half-wedge telemark. Pick a gentle, packed slope and push off into the fall line. Move from a straight parallel run into a telemark by *stepping* your front ski into a stem. That's right. Step the front ski not only into the lead but with the ski stemmed, steering it into a new turn.

When stepping the front ski in a stem across the hill, you will be into your turn quickly. Brace your weight against the edge of the front ski and *quickly* step the rear ski alongside it, edging the snow hard with the uphill edge of your rear ski. "Sting" the snow with the rear ski as you put it down. I like to count to myself: "one (front step), two (rear step)," and so on (see illus. 46).

Now add a pole plant, stinging the snow with your downhill pole *as you sting the snow with the edge of the rear ski.* I think: "one, sting, one, sting; one (front step), sting (rear step and pole plant), one, sting, one, sting." Practice it on the flats at slow speeds. It feels as though you are "walking" down the hill, checking your speed with each ski/edge sting. With a little practice you can walk down anything—steeps, bumps, catchy crud. Remember, the rear ski controls your speed, so edge it fast and hard with your little toe when you step it around.

It's not the most elegant technique, but the step-telemark is a god-send for controlling your speed in hairy situations. The more tools like jump turns and step-teles that you learn the more fun you'll have when the skiing's not perfect.

A HYBRID TURN

Telemarks are indispensable in cruddy snow, very deep powder, crust, or any condition that yanks your feet back as momentum drags your body forward. But parallel turns are often more secure on hard and refrozen snow, when falling forward is less likely but side-to-side stability is elusive. There's a hybrid turn that combines the advantages of both—what I call the *early lead change*. The turn begins with a telemark and, using an early lead change, finishes with a parallel. This is a smooth, elegant turn.

Why a hybrid? Smoother lead changes, more carving, and more stability. The parallel turn finish, with uphill ski advanced, puts you in the perfect position for a telemark turn initiation with a simple change of edges. You don't have to swap feet. It's the best of both worlds, using the tele at the initiation where you need the stability fore-to-aft, and the parallel at the finish where you need stability side-to-side.

Back to your practice slope. Warm up with some of your classic teles. In this maneuver your lead is changed between turns, just as you finish one and start the next. It's as though you are shuffling from turn to turn. The skis are across the fall line when you change leads.

Next, try changing the lead *earlier*. Start the first turn with a telemark, standing tall and steering your skis into the fall line. As your skis find the fall line, *slide the rear ski forward. Keep it weighted and edged as long as you can, until it passes the other foot,* ahead in the parallel "lead." Shift your weight to your outside ski in the parallel turn finish.

The sensation is as though you are "collecting" your skis and knees as your skis come out of the fall line. You may think of it as *driving your rear thigh forward,* or *through,* into an alpine stance. Again, keep that ski weighted until the split-second it comes under you, the transition from the tele lead to the parallel lead.

Notice in the sequence of illustrations how the telemark lead disappears and the turn is finished alpine style (see illus. 47). You check your speed facing downhill in anticipation of the next turn. With the advanced uphill ski of the parallel turn, you have the proper lead to smoothly and quickly initiate a new telemark by simply rolling your knees and edges into the fall line. There's no need for a strenuous lead change into a new tele.

With practice you will find this earlier lead transition much smoother and quicker than changing your lead between turns. It's not meant to replace the smooth, classic "cruising" telemark but rather to add another turn variation to your repertoire.

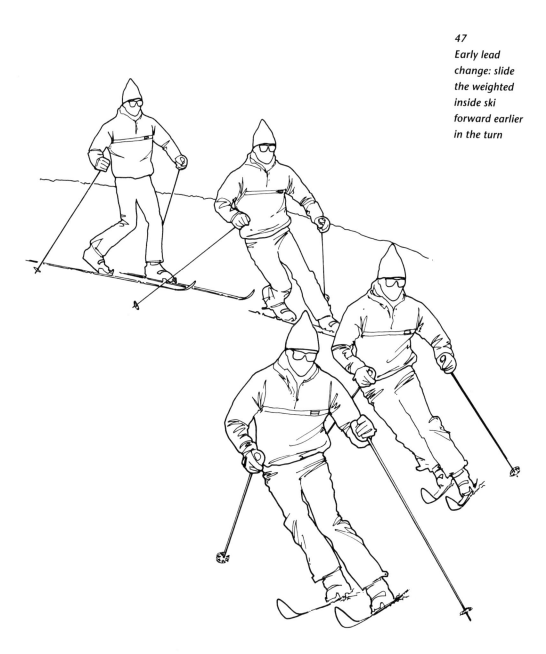

47
Early lead
change: slide
the weighted
inside ski
forward earlier
in the turn

SKIING FROM
THE WAIST UP

A number of years ago Yvon Chouinard and I traveled to Japan to ski on the island of Hokkaido. What a place to ski! Hokkaido was enjoying its usual bumper winter with an abundance of cold, fresh powder. We toured all over the island, chauffeured by a stately, elderly Japanese friend who would sneak away to soak in the nearby hot springs while we beat ourselves up on the slopes.

Skiing in Japan was a different experience. It's rare when recreational skiers in Japan venture off the piste. At the top of each lift, only a short walk would bring us to acres of virgin snow. The best slopes were serviced by odd little single chairs—the Japanese are very private people. In a chair no larger than a dinner plate for my American-sized seat, I clung to the bar, looking for more untouched terrain and those perfectly spaced Japanese trees.

I remember well an out-of-the-way little spot at the large Niseko ski area, a gully with heavy, deep snow topped with a desperate wind crust. It was difficult. If you hesitated the least bit between turns your skis wouldn't come around. Both Yvon and I became possessed with the idea of skiing this crud, caught up in the aggressive attitude it demanded. You had to plant your pole as firmly as the snow allowed and *totally* commit your upper body down the hill. A loud grunt was the perfect signal to begin each new arc.

Typically polite and austere, our Japanese ski partners didn't know what to think about the two Americans fanatically grunting down the desperate slope, riding up on the dinner plate, and going back again. They would follow us politely, quietly face-planting in the treacherous conditions. But finally even Japanese patience succumbed. Exasperated, they tried it, first grunting tentatively, then aggressively, as they committed their bodies to the fall line and their turning efforts began to work.

Bob Mazeri carves corduroy

138

48
*Look farther
down the hill*

moving as though it were joined only by a ball-and-socket or universal joint. Anticipation is an "attitude," not a twisting, of the torso. It's as simple as where you are looking, where you are going.

To achieve this freedom expert skiers combine *all* of the basic points of anticipation. They use their eyes, torso, arms, shoulders, and pole plants together. Each one of these elements is important from the beginning. Experts always go back to them. They use them as a way to cure bad habits or as a focal point for a difficult descent.

FOCAL POINTS

The upper body reflects a skier's "attitude" on skis. Timid skiers may stand very square over their skis, afraid to face the fall line. Defensive skiers even lean and twist up the hill to avoid the fall line.

What you are *thinking* about when you ski can really affect the attitude of your upper body. Below, I've listed a few focal points that I use to get my upper body facing and floating down the fall line.

♦   Think of your shoulders as an artificial horizon on an instrument panel of an airplane. Try to keep that artificial horizon level with the horizon of the snow slope.

◆ Think of your chest as having a headlight (see illus. 49). Pick a target down the hill in the fall line and point that light at the target. As you make turns, keep your light on the target without veering from side to side.

◆ Think of facing the *outside* of the turn—down the hill—rather than the inside (see illus. 50). That means that if you are turning right, try to face the outside of that turn: left. That will get you facing down the hill.

◆ Think of your navel as though it has a string running from it. As you link your turns, imagine someone pulling you down the hill with that string. Let the string pull you; don't pull against it. The feeling, the focus, is *weightlessness* as you allow gravity's string to pull you down the fall line. Moving this direction is the *three-dimensional*

49
Think of your
shoulders as
an artificial
horizon; think
of your chest
as having a
headlight

50
Face the outside
of the turn

movement that I've talked about—not just standing up vertically, but *extending* and moving the body down the hill.

These different focal points will help you with your upper body's attitude and the flow of your turns. Be sure to use them one at a time; more than one is too confusing.

POLING

Back in the old days skiers used one pole like an outrigger, leaning on it for balance and dragging it between their legs as a brake. Then for about eighty years or so, skiers skied with two poles. Today, Norwegians, especially, have reintroduced their heritage and often practice with one pole. Other countries influenced by the Norwegians have caught on to one pole, too. It's a fun thing to try, although in this book I'm going to stick with two poles, the most practical arrangement for propulsion and timing.

To use your poles properly your *poles must be the right length.* For down-hill skiing, whether alpine or telemark, alpine-length poles are the best choice. When touring, your poles should be longer for additional "push" on uphills and flats.

An excellent solution for backcountry skiing, where the terrain goes both up and down, is a pair of adjustable poles that telescope from alpine to nordic touring length. You can adjust them long on the flats and up-hills, short on the downhills, and two different lengths on long traverses.

Poles and Balance

Once you get your pole length straightened out, specific poling exer-cises can improve your technique. You can eliminate your dependence on poles for balance and learn to use them primarily for timing and body position.

Here is an old alpine exercise especially useful for tele skiers who de-pend on their poles for balance: *hold your poles horizontally across your body* (see illus. 51). In each hand you will have the grip of one pole and

51
Hold
your poles
horizontally
across your
body

the shaft of the other. Hold them with your arms relaxed in front of your chest. Try to keep the poles level with your shoulders. Think of the poles as a carpenter's level, and try to keep the middle bubble even with the snow's horizon.

Removing the crutch of your poles can make you painfully conscious of bad habits. For instance, many telemark skiers have a habit of leaning on their uphill pole. They use a rapid uphill pole plant for balance at the finish of each turn and for propulsion into the next. Once that pole is gone their pole-check becomes a butt-check. If you feel that without your poles you are falling uphill too much, *put more weight on your back foot in the little-toe area at each turn's finish, and don't lean into the hill.* (Note: don't carry your car keys in your back pocket.)

Once you feel comfortable linking tele or parallel turns without poles, you can let the poles drop to a normal position. Keep your hands in the same spot as when holding your poles across your body—within your peripheral vision. You don't need to plant the poles; simply find a comfortable position for your hands, poles pointing behind you.

Poles and Timing

Poles are put to good use by timing your turns. A proper pole plant stores energy and regulates the release of that energy into the next turn.

Practice turn timing. Tap the snow lightly with the *downhill* pole before you start each turn. Then turn your skis around the hole you've made in the snow. Think *tap, turn, tap, turn, tap, turn* (see illus. 52). Plant only the *downhill* pole for each new turn. Planting the downhill (inside) pole may be contrary to some region's telemark dogma, but double poling or planting only the uphill pole only reinforces bad habits.

Uphill pole plants lean and rotate your body uphill into the slope— the wrong way to be facing. Some skiers use double pole plants for security in that unstable transition between turns. For some quick-footed skiers these pole plants work—especially when making tight turns in big, steep bumps. But for others this habit squares the body on the skis so that quick turning requires propulsion off the two planted poles—a difficult feat in soft snow. That's why we'll practice single pole plants.

Remember when practicing your poling that it requires timing—an elusive skill dependent on feel and image rather than conscious thought. If you get confused while practicing this skill, do something else. Watch good alpine skiers and imitate their poling movements. Follow a good skier, planting your pole in the same spots that he or she plants and turning your skis in the same tracks. *Don't think.* Try to *see* and *feel.*

52

Think tap, turn,

tap, turn . . .

Different Poling for Different Turns

Watch good alpine skiers and you will notice that their hands stay comfortable and controlled. Hands help create the right attitude for the rest of the body. Hold your arms comfortably flexed, not outstretched, *keeping your hands in front of you in the periphery of your vision* (not down by your hips).

When cruising and making larger-radius turns, a pole plant is used primarily to position your body and signal the edge change for the next turn. There is a relaxed, flowing transition between turns. You swing the pole forward for a gentle pole "touch" as you *rise up* into the new arc (see illus. 52). With these big turns you're probably skiing fast, so the pole plant should be gentle, not a firm sting or gouge that might slow you down. These are the easiest pole plants to mimic and learn. It's the short-radius pole plant that usually needs more attention.

Drop some-thing?

In short-radius turns, especially on steeper terrain, you want to *decel-erate*, not *ac*celerate. Applied in the split-second transition between quick turns, the pole plant becomes a braking technique. It is firm and decisive at the end of the *downward* movement of your body as you finish the turn and begin the next. It's a *sting* of your pole tip and ski edges *at the same time:* simultaneously stinging the snow with edges and the down-hill pole *before* moving into the new turn. It feels quick and aggressive (see illus. 53).

53
The short-
radius pole
plant is an
aggressive
sting

54
Your pole swing should match the radius of your turn; a subtle move of the wrist

To get your pole forward in time for this sting, you'll have to *swing* it forward. Usually your "pole swing" matches your turn radius; in the case of the short-radius turn, it's quicker and more pronounced. The pole swing is a subtle movement at the wrist (see illus. 54).

Your pole plant sets you up for short-radius turns. It's a move crucial to making the skis come around easily in otherwise difficult snow. With the pole basket planted down the hill, the planted pole pushes back against your arm and shoulder and forces your upper body to face downhill. The body twist created by this "blocking" movement stores energy in contracted and stretched muscle groups. When you release this energy into the next turn, your skis are launched into the arc with minimal effort. Whether in heavy crud or light powder, it's the best trick for rhythmic, well-linked turns.

Think of your poling as though you are opening a door for your torso to move through. The door opens *into the next turn* (see illus. 54 and 55).

55
The pole plant
opens the door
down the hill
(parallel turn)

In short turns, that means the door opens directly down the hill—plant your pole downhill, below the boot. In longer turns, the pole plant is more across the hill. Plant the pole more ahead, toward the ski tip.

For some skiers, this idea of *where* to plant the pole is easiest. Notice where the pole is planted in the short-radius turns in the last illustration. The skier's pole is planted clear back by the heel of the boot—between the heel and the fall line (see illus. 55). This helps frame the door for the next turn. Plant the pole farther back toward the heel for short turns, farther ahead toward the ski tip for longer turns.

A different image will help prevent your hands from dropping be-hind—a common error that leans you into the hill. Once you plant your pole, focus on *punching the poling hand forward and "over" the pole*. On steeps, exaggerate this idea, *punching your poling (downhill) and uphill hands down the hill.* Resist the temptation to let your hands—especially your uphill hand—fall behind or drop low by your hip. Keep your hands moving *forward*, down the fall line.

Poling in Crud

Subtle hand movements can work wonders to bring your skis around in thick conditions. I mentioned earlier that the inside hand on the planted pole moves forward, over the pole. The outside (uphill) hand will also aid your turning—especially in difficult snow.

Try it in crud: as you move aggressively into a telemark or parallel turn, throw your outside hand sharply up and forward, down the hill. See in the illustration how the inside pole is planted while the outside hand is moving up and forward (see illus. 56).

56
Raise your outside hand up and forward as you plant your pole

Remember that this is an exaggeration to magnify your movements in difficult snow, where it works great. It is unnecessary on buffed piste.

Inside hand, outside hand. You can't think about it all at once. As I mentioned before, when you get confused, don't think about anything. Poling is mostly a matter of timing, a technique that is easier to ape than describe. Find a good alpine skier whose moves you can mimic.

CROSSOVER

Momentum. Flowing with gravity. That's the sign of a true expert, the skier who seems to move effortlessly down the steepest slopes in perfect control.

Appearances are deceiving. Watch really good skiers making short turns down some steep, narrow path and it will look as though their upper body is completely "quiet," motionless. It's no wonder that instructors teach and students construe the torso's attitude as a *position*. It's so calm it looks almost static. But don't be fooled by that steadfast appearance. Like your feet, the torso is *alive*, moving aggressively toward the next turn. The trunk isn't behind, following the legs. It's not rotating side to side. It's not just on top of the legs. It's *leading*, moving down the hill in a much straighter line than the skis.

This concept is a much more advanced form of anticipation. The point is, this anticipation isn't just a static position, "facing" down the hill. All of my focuses and exercises are to get you facing the right direction, but the end goal is dynamic and fluid. Notice how, in illustration 57, the upper body follows a much straighter line than that of the skis. Like the track that your skis follow, this body line varies according to your turn radius. Usually, the tighter the turn radius, the straighter the line your body will take. In short-radius turns there's simply no time for your heavy torso to follow the serpentine path of your skis.

Most ski instructors call this *crossover:* the upper body crosses over the skis; or you can look it as *crossunder:* as your torso floats aggressively down the fall line, your skis swing back and forth *underneath*.

Following such a line with the torso requires aggressive movement down the hill. While your skis are snaking back and forth under that "floating" trunk, your stomach, back, and buttocks are stretching and contracting, storing and releasing energy into each successive turn. It's a workout. There's nothing quiet or static about it.

Try an exercise that helps crossover in medium-to-long turns: moving your torso into each new turn sooner, while your skis are finishing

57
The line
followed by
the upper
body is much
straighter
than the line
of the skis

the last turn. It's a very dynamic feeling, as your skis race in one direction across the hill while you commit your upper body to the opposite direction, into the *next* turn.

On your practice slope, as your skis come across the slope toward the finish of a turn, plant your downhill pole and move your *whole torso* toward a new one (see illus. 58). Your skis will go one way while your upper body moves the other. It seems unlikely, but your skis miraculously snap around, finishing the last turn crisply and rebounding toward the new one. It's a similar feeling to the "stepping on the uphill ski earlier" that we did in Advanced Parallel Tips.

You might feel as though your torso leads dangerously beyond a balanced position. The payoff is that your skis seem to flatten and turn automatically. This is what we're all after.

When telemarking with this focus you'll develop a "wind-up" effect, twisting the body like a spring, storing energy to release and snap you into the next turn (refer back to illus. 54). In parallel turns you will feel your weight shift to the uphill ski before the ski is steered into a new turn.

OK, try another focus, this time for short-radius turns. Remember earlier when I said to think of a string in your navel, pulling you down the fall line with each turn? Now try moving ahead of the string, keeping it slack: rather than being *pulled* along, be more proactive and move your belly button directly down the fall line into each new turn. Don't hold back; move that belly button straight down the hill. It's the same idea: moving the torso dangerously ahead of everything else.

Parallel or telemark, the fluid movements that come from these exercises preserve the momentum of the upper body rather than slowing it. In parallel turns, they go hand in hand with the exercises that we've worked on throughout this book—especially pointing your knees. In telemarks, they go hand in hand with the early lead change. In either kind of turn, the feeling of a weightless body that isn't resisting the pull of gravity is one of the most elegant sensations of descent on skis.

58
*Move toward
the new turn
as you plant
your pole*

Skiing on One Ski

By the side of the tracks, snow monkeys peered into the train, envious as we munched away at the contents of our bento boxes. The little cog train wound its way into the Japanese Alps toward Shiga Kogen. Along the way, little one-lift ski areas with blown snow were covered with acres of antlike skiers. Our buddies from Tokyo met us at the station after the long ride and ushered us off to the evening's festivities.

I've never understood how, in a culture so reserved as the Japanese, party goers can politely drink until they fall over. This instance was a prerace meeting of the Japanese Telemark Association. Years ago on our first trip, this group had consisted of a few crusty old backcountry skiers and Eiger climbers with missing fingers, drinking ceremoniously through the night. It was now a rowdy bunch of pumped-up racers. There was a hysterical beer-swilling contest, prizes, awards, and, of course, complimentary bottles of Wild Turkey (a race sponsor) for dignitaries. I killed a potted plant with my bottle.

The next morning, while the race was getting organized, Yvon Chouinard, our buddy Fuji, and I went out for a little powder exploration. As usual in Japan, no one was skiing off-piste. Everyone was too polite to tell us not to go. Within 2 hours Y.C. and I knew the trees better than the ski patrol. It was cool skiing: 18 inches or so on a rock-hard rain crust. At the finish of each powder turn, with a little oomph, you could hit the crust and get a great slalom-type rebound into the next face shot. Powder/trees/slalom/HAI!

We'd poached long enough and headed for the race course. The course had two huge pro jumps that looked like auto-exhibit podiums at a car show. Huge. I laughed at the folly of telemark racing—"Stupid racers . . . who would want to fly off of that thing onto a rock-hard landing?" Ten seconds later, Yamura-san skied up and said that I was to fore-run the race. At least 200 people would be watching and, of course, I was a famous telemark skier and would do well and not lose face. Oh, my head.

Numerous turns into it, trying to carry maximum speed, I gritted my teeth and tried to suck up the huge jump. Of course, I was going way too fast and, at the lip,

59
*Skiing on one
ski: hold your
other ski off
the snow*

popped so much air that I flew over the next gate, flag at my ankles. I touched down and desperately pulled off a couple of white-knuckled alpine turns before the finish. The crowd went wild, thinking that "Papaka"-san had popped air and arced a few alpine carves not out of desperation, but as a demonstration.

In the race that followed, that jump caused a lot of carnage. Awards were presented for the most air, the most air upside down, and the most desperate groin-tweaking recovery. No one lost face.

Once again in the festive mode, my hosts asked me to do a clinic. I sneaked off with a bunch of the racers on one of the many bulletproof trails. They were all superb piste skiers. Every exercise, every turn that I demonstrated, they performed flawlessly, the first time, better than I could. Wanting to show them something new, I racked my brain for something that they couldn't do.

The light went on: skiing on one ski. These guys were all used to steppy, sequential racing arcs. I figured that they weren't likely to have been practicing on one ski.

A chorus of polite Japanese guttural "auhoouhooos" accompanied me as I skied down through the group, demonstrating short-radius turns on one foot. Eyes got very big. I pantomimed that they should try; the video rolled, cameras clicked, and the giggling started.

Success.

My Japanese class eventually caught on, and they were fascinated how this exercise emphasized the weight and edge on what normally would be their inside ski for half of their turns. Skiing on one ski is difficult. It's an excellent exercise for edging, using the inside ski and balance maneuvers that come in handy with the unexpected.

Try it. Pick a soft, easy slope, stand on your stronger leg, and try to make a few lefts and rights on that stronger side. Hold the other ski up off of the snow (see illus. 59). I can't give you much more description. You'll have to try.

Do you find yourself lurching around to get that ski to turn on its outside edge? There is a trick: your ankle. Give it your undivided attention. Flex your ankle from the inside corner of your boot (as in a normal parallel turn), to the outside corner of your boot to make that trickier uphill turn (see "The Inside Corner" in Advanced Parallel Tips). You should feel the outside edge under the little-toe side of your foot.

Practice these turns until you can do them on both sides. Now, put both feet on the ground and see what happens. Do you feel how independent your feet are, how "mobile" you've become? Feel that uphill edge? Are you more confident with the inside ski?

Once you get the hang of it, your feet become much more independent. You'll find that using that ankle to edge your uphill ski improves the edging of the downhill one. You'll find that you can edge your back (uphill) ski better in a telemark. The end result is more carve, less skid.

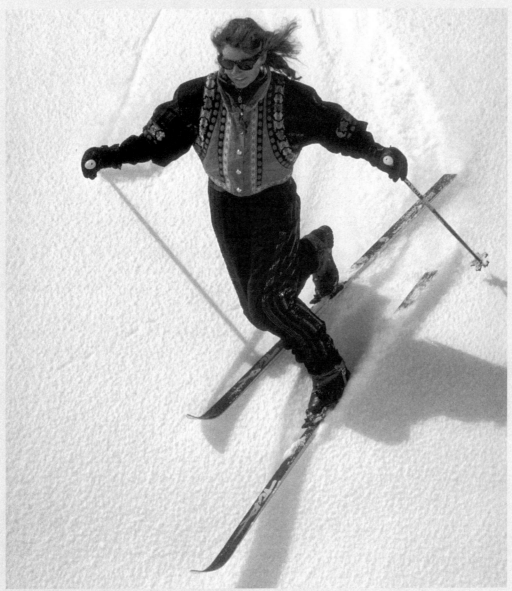

Franziska Witmer-Shapiro works her inside ski

POWDER

Slow-motion grace, effortless movement. Cold, light snow bubbling over my head and pressing sensuously against my body. That's what I feel when I hear the word *powder.*

The locals wait for it. Tentative skiers avoid it. It isn't always effortless, but it's ultimate.

Powder skiing requires proper technique. The snow changes frequently from turn to turn. It weighs heavily on your skis when the sun beats down. It grows dense and perilous with pounding wind.

The resistance of powder snow can give you a false sense of security. You feel as though you don't have to finish your turns because the snow slows you down. But you'll find that as the terrain steepens you'd better finish your turns round and controlled or you're quickly out of control; and unlike on a groomed slope, you can't simply steer your skis sideways to scrape off speed, unless you want to head-plant. You must control your speed with the arc of your turn, flexing your skis from the very start to the very finish of each turn. Learn to turn your skis in round, complete arcs and you'll have the technique for the ultimate powder runs, the real steep and deep.

STARTING OUT IN POWDER

Most skiers have so little opportunity to ski powder that it takes them years to learn how. Unless you live at one of a handful of those legendary deep-snow areas, there is too little of it for consistent practice. There are, however, a number of points of focus that with practice will help you hone your powder skiing as quickly as possible. These ideas have been covered before; they apply to both parallel and telemark skiers:

- Get the feel of equal weight distribution between your skis.
- Strive for equal edging as well as equal weight.
- Use your entire range of motion, with a strong emphasis on extension and flexion of the legs.
- Aggressively move your body down the hill toward the next turn. This is the ultimate move that is a key to expert powder skiing.

More Verbier powder

I'll start with the first idea. It's worth noting for this practice that even if you are an expert piste skier it's best when practicing powder technique to stay clear of rocks and trees. Find a gentle, open slope—ideally one that is covered with a blanket of light, fresh snow. Start by practicing straight running. Once you build a little speed, shift your weight from one ski to another. Quickly you will feel how weight is best distributed between your feet. (In a parallel it's even, like a telemark.) Make some straight runs in the flats and get the feeling of this equal distribution.

Now, still without turning, start moving up and down. You can practice this with your feet in a parallel position or by switching tele leads if you're working on your teles. You should use a bouncing rhythm, standing tall and sinking, extending and flexing. If you're tele skiing think of sinking between your feet. This is a good way to start any powder run, feeling the snow for its resistance and consistency.

Are you comfortable with your weight distribution? Then try a turn: while rising (tele or parallel), press hard on your feet and twist them into a turn. Some describe this as "grinding" their heels (and forefoot in a tele) into the turn. Rise with your body, pressing as you twist your feet, grinding into the cold, light snow. It's easiest to practice one turn at a time, turning into the hill to a stop. Can you feel how your skis flex into an arc, scribing a turn?

Note the difference in your footwork between parallels and teles: in a parallel stance you're pushing both of your heels away from you evenly; in a telemark you're grinding on the inside heel of your front foot and on the ball of the rear foot (little-toe side). For telemark skiers the rear ski is crucial, so be conscious of exerting plenty of weight on that back ski. Use the early edging and steering motions I described in Advanced Telemark Tips.

To link your turns you will have to add the other half to the extension of your legs: a flexion, a sinking motion, relaxing and contracting your legs as you finish each turn. It makes sense. Without sinking, you can't rise again into another arc. Extension and flexion is the distinctive up-and-down technique you see in the films—skiers elegantly using both ends of their range of motion, high and low.

Rise sharply and press your feet away from you to initiate either a telemark or a parallel turn. As your skis come out of the fall line sink and twist your feet into the turn finish. You won't have to try very hard. The resistance of the snow will help finish your turn, pulling your skis further around as you twist your feet, pushing them up and flexing your legs as the pressure builds under your skis. Don't resist; relax your legs as this pressure builds, letting the snow do the work for you. This automatic flexion, and letting the snow do the pushing, is why powder skiers call their favorite turns "effortless."

Gain some speed on your gentle slope, rising and pressing with your feet to start the turns, sinking as you turn your feet into the finish. When you feel the bouncy rhythm add a pole plant at the lowest point of each bounce. This will punctuate each turn, setting you up for a rise into your next one. In this case it's OK—in fact it's best—to exaggerate the up-and-down and pole-plant punctuation.

DEALING WITH THE STEEP AND DEEP

So what about the steep and deep we hear so much about? There are tricks for teles or parallel turns that you should always keep available:

- Reread the last item about rhythm and bounce. Try to see that up-and-down rhythm in your mind's eye. Watch Warren Miller movies, ski-school videos, cable TV, and good skiers under the lift. Use any visual trick that gives you an image of that loose, bouncy rhythm.
- Face down the hill. I know I've said it many times, but you really need to do it here. Face those arms, chest, and navel right down the hill as though you're perfectly confident that your turns will happen. Telemark skiers have to exaggerate this body twist because it's much harder to face the fall line with the rotated hip of the telemark.
- Exaggerate your flexion and extension. At this stage it will feel like an up-and-down movement. Stand taller and sink lower than you think is possible. Rise sharply to emphasize the "pressing away" of your feet, flexing your skis as soon as you begin the arc. Compared with how you feel during your piste turns, *you will feel like you are rising earlier in the turn and sinking longer* (see illus. 60).
- Sharply raise your outside hand up and forward as you rise in order to emphasize your body's extension.
- Don't lean in. Leaning into the hill is the nemesis of powder skiers.
- Practice garlands on steeper slopes, turning into the hill to a stop. Practice your turns in both directions. Exaggerate that early extension of your feet into the turns, then sink as your skis come out of the fall line.

FALL-LINE TURNS

The crux on the steeps certainly isn't turning into the hill to a stop. It's turning *into the fall line*. This time we'll link some turns.

As your skis come out of the fall line and you feel the resistance of the snow slowing you down, *relax your legs*. Let the snow push your feet up

60
*Exaggerate
your flexion
and extension
in powder*

into the turn finish. The powder's resistance will help you sink through the turn and push your feet upward to automatically flex your legs (see illus. 60).

As the snow pushes your skis up and around, it packs into a platform under your feet. Reach down the fall line and plant your pole to signal the next turn. At the split-second that you plant that pole, edge both skis sharply—imagine a gentle *sting* with the pole plant and edges. Now you're committed. Keeping your legs relaxed, "roll" your skis off the platform and into the next turn.

Parallel skiers should think of rolling both skis in the parallel position. Tele skiers should think of rolling and switching leads. I like to think of starting a turn by rolling onto the inside edge of my new back foot—the "making smoother turns" exercise that we worked on earlier in the chapter Advanced Parallel Tips. Whether you're doing a parallel or a tele, as your skis roll toward the fall line, *move your body aggressively into the next turn:* extend your legs, rise sharply, and raise your outside hand to emphasize the extension.

As your skis drop off the platform they'll be very light. Try to make them heavier with your extension and bend them into an arc. Think "heavy feet." Think about keeping them deep in the snow. "Reach" down the hill with your feet. You'll know it the moment you feel it—that weightlessness as your skis drop off the platform and your body's complete extension as your feet reach for the snow below.

WEIGHT DISTRIBUTION AND OTHER FOCAL POINTS

A bad habit that is hard to break is "sitting back." Once you do that it's too easy to get stuck there in the "back seat." You simply don't have to sit back in powder to keep your tips up. In parallel turns I like to emphasize the weight on the rear two-thirds of my foot from the arch back. In tele turning I emphasize the weight *between* my feet, with plenty of rear-foot pressure.

Just as important as fore-to-aft weight distribution in powder is your weight distribution from side-to-side. In deep snow parallel skiers *weight* and *edge* both skis much more evenly than on packed slopes. Many refer to this equal weighting as "skiing two skis as one" (see illus. 61). Telemark skiers weight and edge both skis, too (see illus. 62). If you don't weight and edge both skis you will have all sorts of problems: the splits, crossed tips, or high-speed figure-elevens. If you step your turns around you'll have similar troubles. Beware. You must weight *and* edge both of your skis simultaneously as you initiate each turn. For me, the best focus is the one mentioned earlier in this section and earlier in the book in both Advanced Telemark Tips and Advanced Parallel Tips: think of the inside (uphill) edge of your rear ski as the first thing to touch the snow.

61
*Edge both
skis equally,
whether making
parallel or
telemark turns*

Notice how I keep talking about parallel turns. Yes, free-heel parallels are possible in powder. Sure, it's intimidating to try to turn in deep snow without sticking that leading ski ahead for security. But if you want to practice parallels, just find good powder that's not too deep or grabby, and weight both skis equally. Try to make as many parallel turns as you can, and when you get in trouble drop into a tele. You'll soon find that you won't have to make that survival tele. You'll be looking for opportunities to powder parallel.

A good exercise to review if you're working on parallel turns is the "inside knee" exercise in the Advanced Parallel Tips that helps you edge both skis equally. (You might think of it as tipping over the skis since you really aren't edging into a hard surface.) As you tip (edge) your skis into each new turn, *focus on pointing your inside knee in this new turning direction.*

Telemarkers can weight both skis evenly by emphasizing pressure on the back foot. Tuck your rear leg snugly under you. Don't let it trail behind. Be sure to edge both skis simultaneously, moving onto the ball of your rear foot (little-toe side) at the same time—even earlier—that you pressure the big-toe side of your front foot. Yeah, it's "big-toe, little-toe" again (see illus. 62). It will help to go back to the Advanced Telemark Tips chapter to review these ideas.

62
Think "big-toe,
little-toe" in
tele powder
turns to
weight and
edge both skis

   Last, but by no means least, once you're more comfortable with the idea of powder and getting your skis around in it, work on your anticipation. As I said before, it's not just a static facing of the torso down the hill but a dynamic movement of the body into the next turn. At first it's hard to make this aggressive move in powder. Your natural reaction is to rotate defensively, keeping your upper body in the *last* turn rather than moving it into the next one. It feels secure. But what have you got to lose? The snow's soft, and it's easy to stop.

   Try it. Find a slope with soft, forgiving snow, tighten your cuffs and zippers, put on your hat, and go for it. Make yourself move your body into the next turn. Plant your pole as a signal, and move your navel aggressively down the hill into the next turn. *Go for it.* Try the emphasis I used in Skiing from the Waist Up: as your skis come across the hill to finish the last turn, move your upper body in the *opposite* direction. Keep trying and you'll feel it.

   Ah, that weightless feeling of moving your body confidently down the hill toward the fall line. Once you experience that sensation you will have opened the door to truly fun powder skiing.

CRUD SKIING

Most skiers avoid difficult snow. It hurts their knees and their egos. Then there are some like a Swiss friend of mine who claims, "There is no bad snow, just bad skiers." Bull. There is plenty of bad snow. But just because it's bad, just because it's difficult, doesn't mean it's not skiable. "Survival" skiing can provide some of the most rewarding turning there is.

HOP AND HOPE

In soft crud I try to keep my skis *in* the snow as much as possible and ski it like powder, using an exaggerated flexion and extension of my legs. Terrain allowing, I'll use larger-radius turns; speed helps you plow through heavy snow. If it's steeper, I'll use short-radius turns, but I still *try to keep the skis in the snow*. I'm airborne in the fall line, but it's because of the steepness and my skis' rebound, not because I'm jumping them around.

I've emphasized this thought because jump turns are prevalent as a current fad in tele skiing. It's not uncommon to see an enthusiastic tele skier dressed in shorts, long underwear, and knee pads doing the grasshopper down a buffed piste. I don't believe that jump turns are a substitute for carving skis. In fact, if you become too dependent on them, you'll lose the smooth control in a carve that is critical for edge hold on hard snow and for smooth arcs in powder. First learn to arc, saving the jump for when you really need it.

When is that? When the snow is desperate, I do choose to leap and land (hop and hope). What's desperate? Refrozen crud, breakable crust, snow that is just too unpredictable or too dangerous to push through. In those situations, especially with free heels, you are wise to get out of the snow and into the air. Some prefer telemark jump turns; personally I find the "collected" position of the parallel turn the most effective for leaping and landing.

On steeper terrain jump turns aren't difficult; in fact, steepness helps get your skis airborne. The trick to jump turns is timing—much like good poling technique. It's a huge help if you can find a good skier to mimic down the hill.

Martin Jones hopping and hoping in Kasmir

169

PARALLEL JUMP TURNS

Here is the "sequence of events" for parallel jump turns:

- Traverse to gain speed with skis parallel.
- Anticipate the upcoming turn, facing *directly* down the fall line.
- Set your uphill edges to make a platform and *aggressively* plant your pole down the hill.
- Grunt out loud, pushing up hard off of the platform and *sharply raising your outside arm.*
- Suck up your legs, cranking your skis around. Be sure to point your inside knee into the new turn.
- Land with your skis parallel and traverse to the next spot where you want to turn.

Don't worry if you didn't get all of that because I'm going to repeat it. Note that to practice jump turns you should thoroughly understand the chapter on Skiing from the Waist Up. You will need many of the same ideas—skiing tough conditions are where clean technique and good body position really count. Difficult snow is like a magnifier. It emphasizes each unnecessary little quirk in your technique and uses each one against you. You must go back to the basics: shoulders facing down the hill, hands held ahead, pole plants properly timed, and skillful edging.

It's easiest to practice crud turns one at a time. It helps if the slope is a little steeper because your skis are automatically on edge. If you make one turn at a time you can make one turn, regain your composure in a traverse, then make another turn. When making one turn at a time, however, you can't use the energy stored from the finish of the last turn to snap into the next. You'll need a "pre-turn" to set you up for each complete turn: you need to execute a strong sinking, edging, and steering motion before you push off into the new turn. That's the step above that combines the aggressive pole plant and edge set.

OK, we're on the slope. I'll break it down again. Try seeing these moves in your mind's eye:

- Get a bit of speed up and then sink quickly—sink, steer uphill, and edge *both* skis—planting your pole aggressively as you do so (see the top figure in illus. 63).
- Now, extend your legs and stand up abruptly. Push off that platform with *both* feet and launch your body into the air. *Raise your outside arm sharply* to help give yourself more lift. Point your inside knee into the new turn. You can see that move in the second figure of the parallel jump turn illustration.
- Think of your legs as landing gear. As your skis lighten toward the end of your body's upward extension, lengthen your air time by "bringing up the landing gear." Suck up your legs and bring them out of the

snow. With your legs contracted and skis pulled upward, you are now free of whatever catchy snow you are trying to avoid. Point your skis in the desired direction and make your turn in midair.

- Once your skis are turned, lower your landing gear and finish your turn. Reach for the snow with your legs extended so you can absorb the shock as you land. Landing and absorbing with *both* of your legs will store energy for your next leap.

To execute jump turns you must use a strong pole plant. If you plant your pole in the right place at the right time, the wound-up energy in your abdomen and torso will do most of the turning for you. Sound familiar? You must anticipate and be totally committed to each upcoming turn, facing directly down the fall line. Plant your pole in the fall line directly below your boots—clear back by your heel if the slope is steep—not forward toward your tips. This pole-plant position forces your torso to face down the hill and increases the "wind-up" effect. Note the strong pole plants of the first and last figures in the illustration.

The pole plant is a firm, decisive sting that punctuates the end of each turn and the start of the next. Brace your torso with the pole. Your torso will want to rotate through the turn finish, but poling stops this movement and stores the energy in the muscles of your back and abdomen. As you leap up and bring your skis out of the snow, this stored muscular energy launches your skis into the next turn.

TELEMARK JUMP TURNS

In many situations I use parallel jump turns. But if advanced parallel turns aren't in your bag of tricks yet, or if you prefer telemarks, you will want to practice jump-tele turns (see illus. 64). If you are a parallel skier, tele turns will be fun to do for a change. The timing, pole plant, and anticipatory moves of teles are the same as in parallel turns.

64
A jump-tele
turn

The big difference that I find between jump teles and jump parallels is in getting my hips around from one tele to the next while in midair. It takes a lot of *punch*. In some snow I prefer using the telemark "early lead change" (see the chapter More Free-heel Turns) so that I can make the pre-turn in a stable parallel position. Plus, when finishing in a parallel turn you already have the correct lead for initiating the next tele.

Here's the sequence using the classic telemark lead change:

- Traverse in a telemark position, downhill foot advanced.
- Sink and edge—big-toe, little-toe—to make a pre-turn, anticipating with your torso and planting your pole firmly.
- Push up hard off the balls of both feet, raise your outside arm, and move your body into the fall line. Take advantage of the lightening of your skis from your sharp upward movement and change leads by dropping your new inside ski/foot *back*.
- Continue to lighten your skis by sucking up your "landing gear"; turn your airborne skis where you want to go.
- Land in the next tele, ready for your traverse and another turn.

You can also use an earlier lead change in jump teles, which is my preference. The chief difference is in the traverse-and-turn initiation:

- Make the initial traverse in a *parallel stance.*When you sink and edge for your pre-turn, make sure your skis are in a parallel turn finish rather than a tele.
- Push off as in a parallel jump turn, raising your outside arm.
- Once your body is tall, suck your legs up and turn your skis, landing in a tele.
- Tele-turn out of the fall line, quickly sliding the uphill ski forward into a parallel position for your next parallel pre-turn.

It's optimistic to think that you can jump right into difficult snow and practice linked short turns. First practice the proper techniques in an easier situation, not necessarily on groomed conditions but in a better exposure, one with less wind deposition and not so steep. Learn the sensations in this environment. When you jump into harder snow imagine yourself making and feeling the same moves as you did in practice.

Practice the turns one at a time as I have described them. This makes the fall line less intimidating. As your confidence grows try eliminating the traverse altogether. Jump from one turn to another with a "fall-line attitude." At first it's strenuous, but when you get the hang of it you will be able to use the snap in your skis to take much of the effort out of your jump.

Easy to say, I know. With practice, you will find turns of this kind quite easy. Learn the timing, visualize it in your mind's eye, and ski the image that you "see."

MOGULS

For years I refused to ski bumps at the resorts. I would go to great lengths to avoid mogul slopes, ricocheting across desperate traverses in search of groomed or windswept terrain. I rationalized that I was a cruiser. The fact was, I wasn't very comfortable in bumps, so I avoided them.

Although it's easy to visualize skiing the steep and deep, I wasn't really good at it back then, especially if it wasn't champagne powder. It wasn't until I learned to ski moguls that the steep and deep got easier. Once armed with better mogul technique, those steep shots in the trees became less intimidating to me. Fall-line turns became the norm. They were easier to make exactly where I needed to turn. Because I no longer avoided moguls, my favorite ski areas grew into acres of new terrain.

You don't need to make lightning tele-lead switches and desperate recoveries to be a good mogul skier. Nor do you need to suffer knee-pounding turns when ricocheting off each mogul. Certain points of focus will help you become a smooth, controlled mogul skier who arrives at the bottom, run after run, with limbs and equipment intact. Many of these moves are the same ones you've focused on all along in your free-heel skiing. They are the same skills looked at in a slightly bumpier perspective. Since moguls tend to amplify your weaknesses, these on-piste moves can be key to your off-piste performance.

It's most important to make up your mind that moguls aren't the enemy. Gritting your teeth while aggressively slamming each bump won't make them go away. Yeah, people do it under the lifts run after run. They probably have young knees. Skis bend, buckles break, bindings rip out, headaches throb. Stay light and relaxed and flow with the hill and gravity. Don't fight them. Aggressive skiing doesn't just mean heavy and hard; it also means light and quick.

Something that contributes to that light, quick feeling is rhythm. Visit a resort like Telluride or Taos and you'll find many good bump runs—and little else to ski. No doubt there's lots of other terrain, but the long, unbroken steep slopes that characterize these areas are usually well-endowed with moguls. They may look frightening at first, but remember

Air time

174

that these noteworthy resorts have bumps shaped by expert skiers on long skis. With a relaxed attitude and a little practice you'll find lines through these moguls that are steep but reasonable. Bumps carved with rhythm provide that incredibly exhilarating feeling of weightlessness between turns that is caused by flowing with the pull of gravity.

PRACTICING ON A SMOOTH SLOPE

Let's get on snow. Odd as it sounds, it helps to develop a rhythm for mogul skiing by practicing *out* of the bumps on a smooth, moderately steep slope. Make a series of short-radius turns, confining them to a narrow imaginary "corridor" down the fall line. Better yet, find a single-width snow cat track that goes directly downhill and use it for your corridor. If you finish each turn to control your speed you will soon feel the rhythm you're after.

There are a couple of points of focus that I like to use making these short-radius turns. If your rhythm feels jerky and syncopated, think of your poles as the metronome that punctuates each turn. Remember the short-radius pole plants in the chapter Skiing from the Waist Up? Punctuate each turn finish with a determined pole plant, a *sting,* that times your turn and sets your body up for the next turn. In that same section, review "opening the door" and *where* to plant your pole in short-radius turns (see illus. 65).

Try concentrating on facing down the hill *even more* than you ever have before. How do you face your body down the hill *more?* Skiers refine their movements in increments. "Facing the fall line" is not the same for a skier working on beginning wedge turns as it is for a skier making advanced parallel turn.

Facing the fall line is crucial in moguls. Look down the hill and feel that light, free separation of your upper and lower body. *Your navel, innie or outie, should be pointing straight down the fall line.* Your torso will "float" down the hill while your skis snap rhythmically back and forth to control your speed. Your abdomen, the connector between that floating torso and those active skis arcing back and forth, will feel like it is getting a workout, flexing and extending.

STARTING IN THE TROUGHS

Most skiers agree it's easiest to begin your mogul skiing in the troughs. Look for a moderate-angled mogul slope with small, well-spaced bumps.

65
To develop a rhythm for mogul skiing, first practice your short-radius turns on a smooth slope

Good practice bumps are hard to find. Some tips: look for places where bumps are less likely to grow too large—below obstacles like rocks or trees, or on slopes that are occasionally groomed. Ski on the sides of the run, where bumps are usually better spaced, rather than the middle.

Choose a corridor like the one you used on the smooth slope. Look ahead down the corridor (your "line") and make those same round, controlled turns in the smooth spots between the moguls (see illus. 66). Stay

66
Telemarking in
the troughs

relaxed, and keep your eyes several bumps ahead. Avoid looking down at your tips—this is critical.

The following points will help your mogul skiing. Be sure to think about them *one at a time*. There are a lot of them (see illus. 67).

Feet

Converging or diverging skis can be deadly in a sea of bumps. You've got to edge both skis—tele or parallel—to keep them traveling in the same direction. *Edge both skis simultaneously.* Parallel skiers, think about your inside knee: point it in the direction of each new turn. You can

67
Teles in moguls:
think (one at a
time) feet,
shoulders,
abdomen,
hands, poles . . .

actually *lead* with it. Tele skiers, *edge the rear ski first; initiate the turn with it.* Don't make step-turns; try initiating each turn with the rear ski. Review the pointy-knee and back-ski points in Advanced Parallel Tips or Advanced Telemark Tips.

Shoulders

If you lean or bank in your turns you might have difficulty getting your skis around. This is a common problem among telemarkers. The symptoms are similar to not facing the fall line: you have good longer turns, but you have difficulty with the short fall-line turns required for moguls. An elegant technique in fast, deep-radius turns, banking will only get you into trouble in the bumps.

Think shoulders. Face them down the hill. It may help to actually *hold your downhill shoulder back* as you plant your pole. This will twist your torso so it faces the fall line, preparing it for the upcoming turn.

Abdomen

As said before, ski with your abdomen. Point your belly button directly down the hill. Review the string-in-the-navel idea in Skiing from the Waist Up. Feel the muscles on the uphill side of your abdomen stretch, the ones on the downhill side contract. Feel those abdominals doing more of the work.

Hands

Moguls can wreak havoc with a skier's hand position. Uphill hands that persistently drop behind twist the body into the hill and set you up for a nasty fall. Try especially hard to keep your hands down the hill and within your peripheral vision. It helps to think of forcing your uphill hand downhill. It's like punching a bag. Push your uphill hand ahead of the downhill one that's planting the pole.

Poles

As you watch good mogul skiers you will notice the aggressive, determined pole plant that signals each new turn. In short-radius turns through bumps, plant your pole at the finish of each turn to coincide with the "sting" of your edges as you check your speed and set up for the next turn. It's the same thing that we practiced earlier in the corridor.

As important as *when* you plant your pole is *how* and *where*. Plant the basket down the hill beneath your downhill foot so that your body is "open" to the upcoming turn. Reach downhill—not toward your tips.

With your skis across the hill, your basket should be back by your heel as you set up for a short-radius turn.

LOG WALKING

An alpine instructor once showed me a trick called "log walking." It works great with either tele or parallel turns. You simply step over the mogul. I know—looking down Tourist Trap at Vail, the idea of stepping over chest-high bumps seems improbable. Trust me. As your ski tips are pushed up by a mogul, step over the top of it with your uphill ski as though the mogul were a log. In a parallel turn step onto your new outside ski and steer it into the fall line. In a telemark, use the bump to slow you as you step over it into your lead change. Tele skiers, *don't forget the rear ski;* come down on *both edges* in your new tele and steer it into the fall line.

Try it. As your skis ride up the bump, quickly step over the top. Alpine skiers will step from one foot to the other—from their current downhill ski to the new outside/downhill ski. Tele skiers will step into a new lead/turn. Exaggerate the movement and you will be log hopping instead of log walking.

It might take more than blithe hopping to get over the tops of huge moguls. You will need more shock absorption with another focus: your knees. I think of "lifting" my knees to absorb an especially large bump. I don't want to wait stiff-legged until the bump shoves my knees up into my chest. It's as though you anticipate each bump in order to soften the blow. Time it right, lift your knees, and you can log walk over even huge bumps.

EXTENDING

Find a skier on the hill who stays low in the bumps. You won't have to look for long because getting low in bumpy situations is a natural reaction. Chances are the skier you're watching will do okay in the first few turns. But he'll soon start getting thrown around and compressed lower and lower until he has nowhere to go. With no more shock absorption he becomes a human projectile ricocheting off each undulation in the terrain. Stuck in the back seat, he's lost his shock absorption by overcompressing his springs—his legs. By *extending your legs* between turns and standing tall, you can stretch those springs to prepare for another compression.

That's the other half of that leg-lifting business: *extending your legs.* Log walking helps because there's a natural extension when you step over something. But if you feel as though you are getting smaller and smaller as you pound down the hill, try extending your legs as you *press your skis into the valley* once you step over the bump. You might think of it as standing up, although it's much more of a leg extension movement than truly standing up.

If you are turning in the troughs, the motion will be the same as in skiing deep snow, when you *press your skis into a new turn* as you drop off your platform. Using parallels, rise over the mogul, press on the balls of your feet, and press your tips down into the trough. In a telemark, keep plenty of weight on that back ski and edge as you press the front ski into the trough. In either turn, you will feel as though your legs are shock absorbers, compressing to absorb the high spots, storing energy, then springing back and extending into the low spots.

Try this exercise: take a shallow traverse across a mogul slope, no turns, absorbing the moguls by pulling up on your knees and then extending your feet into the troughs. Try to *keep your head the same height.* Do the absorbing with your knees and ankles, and keep your head the same height as you traverse the slope.

I find that this "head height" exercise is an especially important one for telemark skiers. Most tele skiers have trained themselves in the telemark lead change to stand up as they change leads. In this exercise, try changing leads as you go over the bumps *without standing up.* You'll need to consciously pull up on your feet so that instead of standing up during this lead change, you absorb the bump. I think of pulling up on my knees, *sneaking my front foot back and back foot forward* in the lead change. As you extend down the other side, instead of standing up, think of letting your *legs get longer.* I know—it's an esoteric idea until you get into moguls or uneven terrain; but it's possible to think of the head being level and, rather than compressing your whole body and then "standing up," thinking of the legs *coming up* to go over a bump, then *extending* into the next low spot.

I think of pulling my legs up under me, then pushing my feet into the trough. For me, even better than thinking of keeping my *head* level is thinking of keeping my *navel* level. Try it: in your bump traverse, flex and extend your legs, keeping your *navel* at the same level (refer back to illus. 67).

Once you feel your body is more "quiet" and your legs are doing the absorption work in this vertical plane, see if you can feel them getting more out to the side in your turns and then coming under you be-tween turns. That's the ultimate step for rounder turns in the bumps. Refer to "Crossover" in the chapter Skiing from the Waist Up for more on this idea.

Each day you venture into the bumps you will find yourself more in tune with your body's position and less intimidated by surprises. You will begin to venture into the bumps purposefully—or at least not go out of your way to avoid them. Your favorite ski area will get bigger, the backcountry easier. Your skiing will improve—even on the steep and deep!

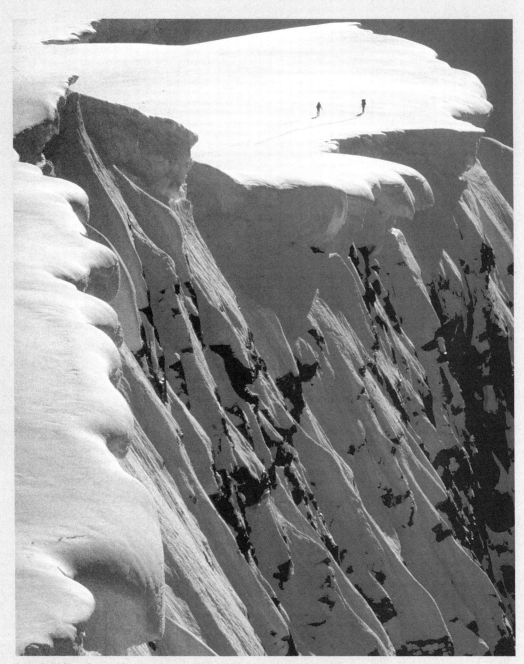

French Ridge above Gloomy Gorge, Mount Aspiring, New Zealand

Jordi

Down from the Haute Route, we sipped a beer in the Zermatt Bahnhofstübe with our Andorran acquaintances from the tour. Andorra is a tiny principality trapped in a mountain cirque between France and Spain. Although they carry French passports, the Andorrans seemed much more like gregarious Spanish or Italians than brooding French. Among their group of five they seemed to speak just about everything: Catalan, their local dialect, and its cousin, Spanish; French, because they carry French passports and work with the French; English to speak to the tight-fisted Brits who frequent their duty-free country; and Italian because . . . why not? It's the best food.

The rowdy Andorrans had just finished the route and were waiting to catch a train. Jordi, the star, was beyond euphoria. A mid-thigh amputee, Jordi had just completed Chamonix-Zermatt on his only leg. He used one ski and outriggers. As far as his friends knew he was the first.

I looked at Jordi and thought back to that long, hot day from Mont Fort (Verbier) to the Cabane du Dix. Four passes. A 4:00 A.M. start with headlamps. Noisy skiing on a rock-hard crust with full hardware: heel lifters, skins, and *harscheisen* (ski crampons). We climbed Rosablanche, dropped into a short, steep couloir to long, perfect corn slopes and the Lac du Dix. The long traverse around Dix was a good thrash over kilometers of avalanche debris. The last climb was a sweltering slog up 3,000 feet to the Dix hut. All afternoon we lolled outdoors re-hydrating, alternately taking sun and trying to get out of it. A typical randonnée afternoon, it was too soft to ski. We dozed, lazy in the warm light and cool breeze of the huge cirque, woozy from the tasteless, priceless French beer.

We knew that Jordi was below us, poling across the debris. He and his friends arrived during dinner. The entire hut (more than a hundred people) evacuated the dining room and cheered him up the final steep slope. Most of us had just done the same tour, on two legs, and we were trashed. Jordi swung up the last step, twisted out of his ski, and collapsed into a seat on the porch. He was still smiling and good-natured. "Sono distrutto," he told me in Italian. "I am destroyed."

The next day he got up early and did it again.

The shorter days were better as one could get off of the snow before it became too soft. For Jordi, on firmer frozen corn, his cramponed outriggers gave great purchase. He had quite a system for climbing: a skin and ski crampon for the ski, and outriggers with crampons that were (tediously) screwed onto their little skis. When climbing on his ski he placed the crampons, leaned on the outriggers, and swung his leg through. On steep, step-kicking climbs he had to carry his ski, use the outriggers like a handrail, and dip up each successive step kicked in the steep snow. A friend in front prepared the steps, a friend in back helped place his foot in difficult spots. Some of these difficult spots had thousands of feet of exposure. Each descent required Jordi's "engineer" friend's removing the screwed-on crampons. When he got his spikes off and started down, you could see how he felt free. The guy flew like a bird.

On the downhill, Jordi was one of the best skiers of the lot, especially in the worst snow. He never seemed to need his outriggers, carving his single ski elegantly through the crustiest conditions. He was so accomplished with this system that I wondered if he had always skied on one leg. After one descent, looking back on his beautiful arcs, he told me his story. At a ski area in Andorra, in thick fog, he had struck a snow cat that was preparing a slope. He lost his smashed leg. He was seventeen when he had his accident; this trip was its tenth anniversary. He had always wanted to do the Haute Route.

BIBLIOGRAPHY

Abraham, Horst. *Skiing Right.* Boulder, Colorado: Johnson Books, 1983.

Hall, Bill. *Cross–Country Skiing Right.* San Francisco: Harper and Row, 1985.

Joubert, Georges. *Teaching Yourself to Ski.* Aspen, Colorado: Aspen Ski Masters, 1970.

Lunn, Arnold. *A History of Skiing.* Oxford: Oxford University Press, 1927.

Tejada-Flores, Lito. *Backcountry Skiing: The Sierra Club Guide to Skiing Off the Beaten Track.* San Francisco: Sierra Club Books, 1981.

Tejada-Flores, Lito. *Breakthrough on Skis: How to Get Out of the Intermediate Rut.* New York: Vintage Books, 1986.

Witherell, Warren, and David Evrard. *The Athletic Skier.* Salt Lake City: The Athletic Skier, Inc., 1993.

INDEX

JOHN WARNER

ABOUT THE
AUTHOR

Paul Parker has been telemark skiing for over twenty years. Formerly a member of the Professional Ski Instructors of America's Nordic Demonstration Team, he is a certified ski instructor in both nordic and alpine disciplines. Involved for many years in the sport's rapidly changing technologies, including boot and ski design, he currently researches and designs skis for TUA Ski and manages ski products for Patagonia. He lives in Breckenridge, Colorado.

THE MOUNTAINEERS, founded in 1906, is a nonprofit outdoor activity and conservation club, whose mission is "to explore, study, preserve, and enjoy the natural beauty of the outdoors. . . ." Based in Seattle, Washington, the club is now the third-largest such organization in the United States, with 15,000 members and five branches throughout Washington state.

The Mountaineers sponsors both classes and year-round outdoor activities in the Pacific Northwest, which include hiking, mountain climbing, ski-touring, snowshoeing, bicycling, camping, kayaking and canoeing, nature study, sailing, and adventure travel. The club's conservation division supports environmental causes through educational activities, sponsoring legislation, and presenting informational programs. All club activities are led by skilled, experienced volunteers, who are dedicated to promoting safe and responsible enjoyment and preservation of the outdoors.

The Mountaineers Books, an active, nonprofit publishing program of the club, produces guidebooks, instructional texts, historical works, natural history guides, and works on environmental conservation. All books produced by The Mountaineers are aimed at fulfilling the club's mission.

If you would like to participate in these organized outdoor activities or the club's programs, consider a membership in The Mountaineers. For information and an application, write or call The Mountaineers, Club Headquarters, 300 Third Avenue West, Seattle, Washington 98119; (206) 284-6310.

Send or call for our catalog of more than 300 outdoor titles:

The Mountaineers Books
1001 SW Klickitat Way, Suite 201
Seattle, WA 98134
1-800-553-4453